The Solar System

THE Sky

Núria Roca & Carol Isern
Rocio Bonilla

BARRON'S

The sky is spectacular

Alice and Oliver are looking at the sky. The Sun comes out early in the morning and the Moon appears at the end of the day.

"And when the sky is dark, it becomes filled with many little dots of light, which are the stars," says Oliver.

Looking very far away

Oliver sees a little dot moving high up in the sky, but he would like to see it better. Is it a planet? A star? A spaceship?

Alice explains to him that if they could go to an observatory, they would be able to look through a telescope, which is a tool that astronomers use to observe the sky.

Astronomy

Astronomers are people who study everything in the sky: the planets, the satellites, and the stars.

Astronomy is a very ancient science. There are many things in the sky, but the astronomers don't know them all yet!

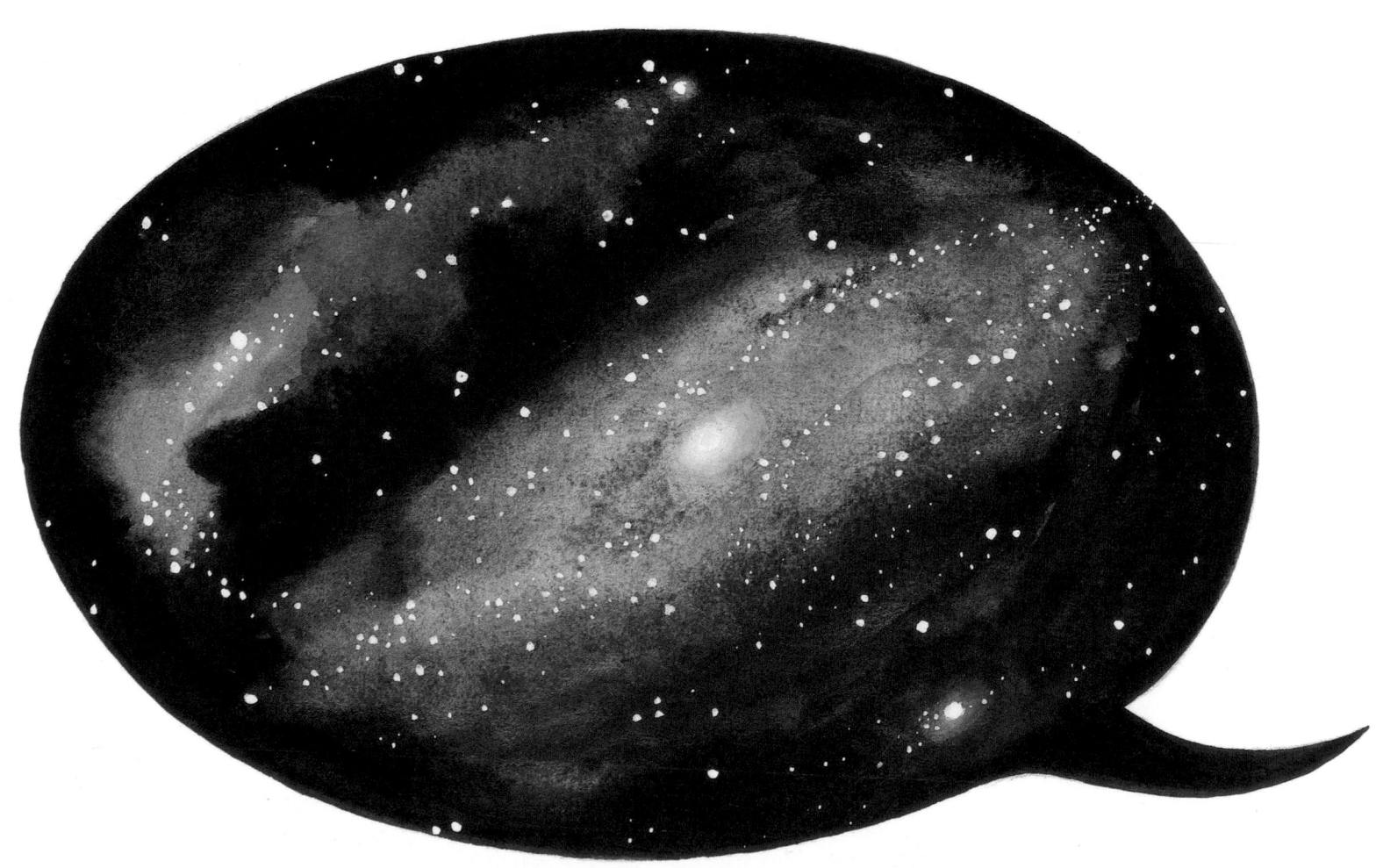

The Earth is round

We used to think that the Earth was flat, but many years ago, we discovered that it is round! If you left your house and kept walking, you would eventually reach your house again, from the other side!

"We would be like two ants walking around a ball!" says Alice.

The Earth dances

The Earth is round and turns like a spinning top.
And at the same time, it revolves around the Sun!

It's like a dancer spinning as she dances around her partner, the Sun! That's why we say that the Earth is a planet. A planet is an astral body that revolves around a sun.

Let's travel!

The Earth is like a spaceship traveling through space. We are the passengers and, although we don't realize it, we also travel through space with it.

Space is very, very large, but the Earth never gets lost: It is always close to the Sun and always follows the same path.

The sky is not the same the whole year 'round

Things in the sky do not move in the same way. For example, in summer the Sun is higher in the sky, warms more, and stays out longer; in winter it is lower, heats less, and sets earlier.

Everything revolves around the Sun

The Earth turns like a spinning top and moves around the Sun. The Moon also turns and revolves around the Earth. There are also many neighboring planets that revolve around the Sun, too.

"Wait a minute, this is confusing! We don't understand anything!" say Oliver and Alice.

The Moon is always with us

"So, does the Moon rotate around the Earth?" asks Oliver.
"Exactly! The Moon is always with us!" says Alice's mother.

The objects that revolve around the Sun are called planets. Objects that revolve around planets are called satellites, such as a moon.

Day and night

If you turn and put your back to the Sun,
your belly is in the shade, right?

Well, this is what the Earth does to the Sun. As the Earth turns, the sunlight reaches one side, but not the other. And that is why we have day and night.

Why do we have winter?

"But that's not all. Imagine that the Earth had a head and feet. When the Earth turns with its feet pointing toward the Sun,

it is winter at the feet. Although the feet are closer to the Sun, the Sun's rays are less intense. At the same time, it is summer at the head. Although the head is farther from the Sun, the Sun's rays are more intense," says Alice's mother.

Where are stars when we can't see them?

During the day, we can't see the stars because the sunlight is so strong that it prevents us from seeing them. It's like trying to see the light from a flashlight on a sunny day.

At night, we can see the planets as well as the stars. "The stars sparkle, but planets don't," says Alice's mother.

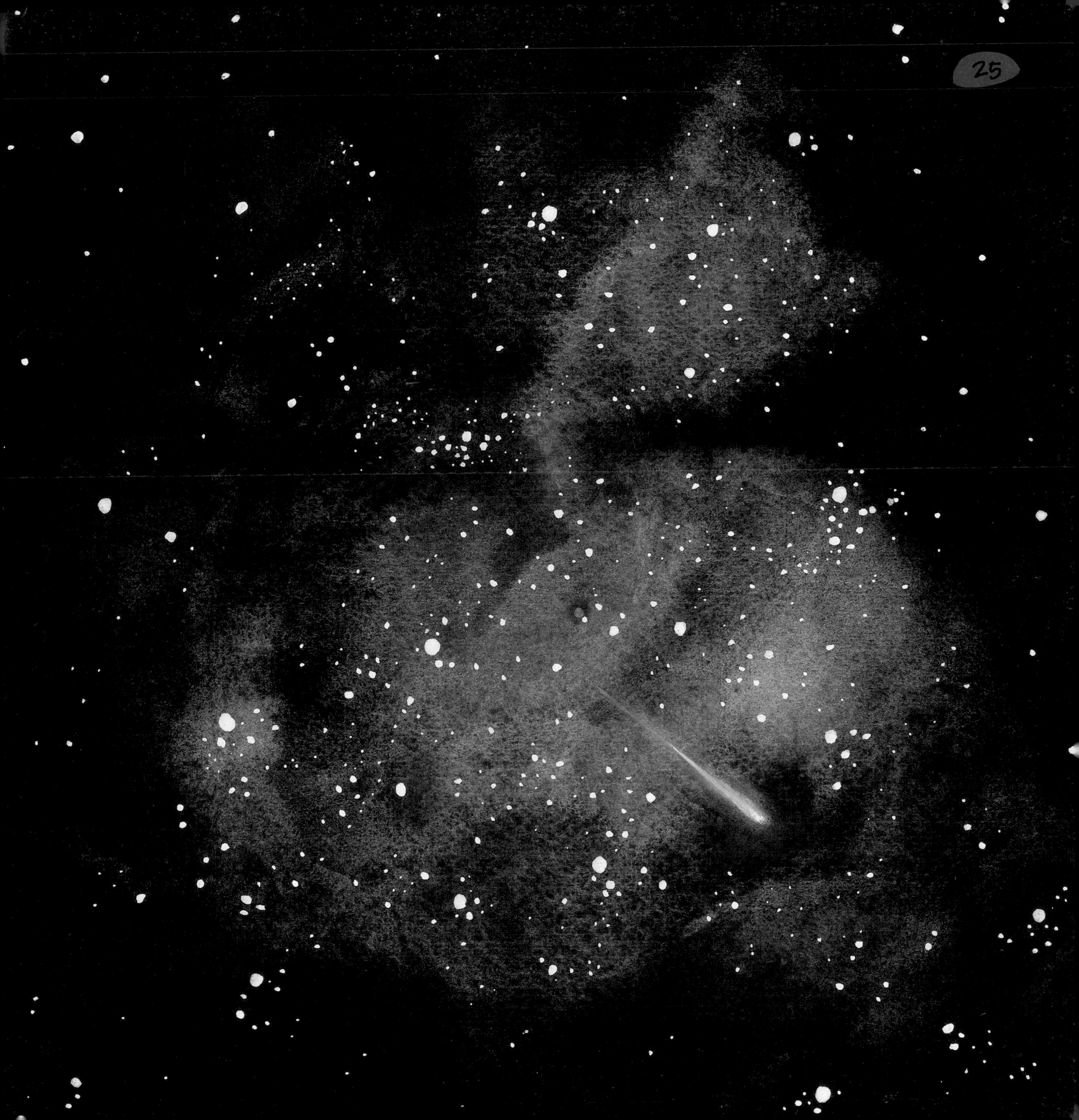

The solar system

Eight major planets revolve around the Sun: Mercury, Venus, Earth, Mars, Jupiter, Saturn, Uranus, and Neptune.

All of these, together with their satellites and other minor planets, form the solar system.

"I want to be the Sun because then the whole world would spin around me!" exclaims Oliver.

Stars

"And what about stars?" asks Oliver, who never tires of asking questions.

"No, stars do not revolve around the Sun. Stars are suns like ours, but they are much farther away than our sun," replies Alice's mother.

A space dance

Our solar system is made up of our sun and eight major planets that revolve around it.

This dance never stops... and it's always the same!
That's how we know when it will be winter and summer,
and when it will be day and night!

Activities

A trip to discover the distances between the planets

You can go on a trip to the countryside with Mom and Dad to discover the distances between the different planets. Take a tape measure with you and find a very open space. It doesn't need to be the size of a football field, but you must be able to run through it. Place a marble at one end of the field to represent the Sun and from there, measure: Mercury, 18 inches (45 cm); Venus, 32 inches (80 cm); Earth, 47 inches (120 cm); Mars, 71 inches (180 cm); Jupiter 20 feet (6 m). If you still have some space left, you can measure: Saturn 36 feet (11 m); Uranus 72 feet (22 m); and Neptune 115 feet (35 m).

Otherwise, just imagine the enormous distance there is between us and our neighbors!

Why do we have summer and winter?

Now we are going to do some craft work. You will need a lamp (such as a flexible table lamp), some modeling clay, a pencil (that you haven't sharpened yet) and an adult (could be Mom or Dad) to help you. With the modeling clay, make a large ball, at least the size of an adult's fist. When you have finished, stick the pencil through it so that it clearly emerges from the bottom part. Then place the ball, which represents the Earth, so that the lamp can shine on it with the pencil slightly diagonal. Look at how the light falls on it: Which zones are illuminated the most? If you move the Earth in a circle around the Sun (the lamp), you will see that inside the illuminated zone there is a lighter part and a darker part. In the darker part, it is winter because the light reaches it with less intensity, therefore, warms it less and it is colder. This means that the seasons change because the Earth changes its position in space in relation to the Sun.

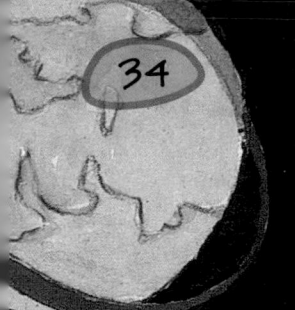

An **astral body** has a specific form, for example: planets, satellites, stars, comets, asteroids, and meteorites.

A **telescope** is the main instrument used by an astronomer for research. It's like a gigantic magnifying glass used for seeing things that are very far away. Thanks to the telescope, astronomers can see the planets, the stars, the satellites, and everything that is in space.

Parent's guide

An **astronomer** is a scientist who studies the sky, the astral bodies, and all the phenomena that take place there, in other words, a scientist who studies astronomy. The astronomer observes the movements of the astral bodies, discovers new ones, and measures the distance between them.

A **star** is an astral body that has its own light, which makes it shine. A **planet** is an astral body that does not have its own light and revolves around a star. In our solar system, the Sun is the star (because it has its own light and that's why it gives us warmth and light), around which the eight planets revolve, one of which is the Earth. A **satellite** is an astral body that does not have its own light either and always revolves around another astral body, such as a planet.

Despite the fact that we see the Sun rise every day in the east and set in the west, and **it seems like the Sun is moving** from one end of the sky to the other, it is not moving, we are. It's like when you go on a rollercoaster: Things pass by very quickly before you, don't they? However, the things are not moving, we are.

During the day, the stars are not visible because the light of the Sun, the star in our solar system, prevents us from seeing the light from stars farther away. It's like trying to see the light from a flashlight in broad daylight on a sunlit terrace.

Proportionally, the **sizes of the astral bodies** in the solar system would be: The Sun, 1 m; Mercury, 3.5 mm; Venus, 9 mm; Earth, 10 mm; the Moon, 3 mm; Mars, 5 mm; Jupiter, 100 mm; Saturn, 80 mm; Uranus, 35 mm; Neptune is like Uranus, but slightly smaller.

THE SKY

First edition for
North America published in 2014
by Barron's Educational Series, Inc.
© Gemser Publications, S.L. 2013
El Castell, 38 08329 Teià (Barcelona, Spain)
www.mercedesros.com
Text: Núria Roca and Carol Isern
Illustration: Rocio Bonilla
Design and layout: Estudi Guasch, S.L.

All inquiries should be addressed to:
Barron's Educational Series, Inc.
250 Wireless Boulevard
Hauppauge, NY 11788
www.barronseduc.com

ISBN: 978-1-4380-0477-8
Library of Congress Control Number: 2014935176

Date of Manufacture: June 2014
Manufactured by: L. Rex Printing Company Limited,
Dongguan City, Guangdong, China

Printed in China
9 8 7 6 5 4 3 2 1

Variations of Knit and Purl Stitch Patterns

The knit and purl stitch patterns in this section are simple to knit yet they produce interesting designs that come out especially well if done with smooth yarn. The patterns vary from simple checks to refined picot, diamond, and cable patterns. It is also worthwhile to experiment with the patterns. For example, the rice stitch pattern on page 22 will produce an interesting tweed effect if you knit it with a multicolor yarn or if each row is worked in a different color. Also, the small patterns make a good background design when used in combination with cable patterns. They will make the cables stand out more.

Tip: Always take a glance at the wrong side of the knitting as well. You may find a new and charming pattern there.

Garter Stitch
Knit all stitches in every row.

Stockinette Stitch
Row 1 (right side row): Knit all stitches.
Row 2 (wrong side row): Purl all stitches.
Repeat rows 1 and 2.

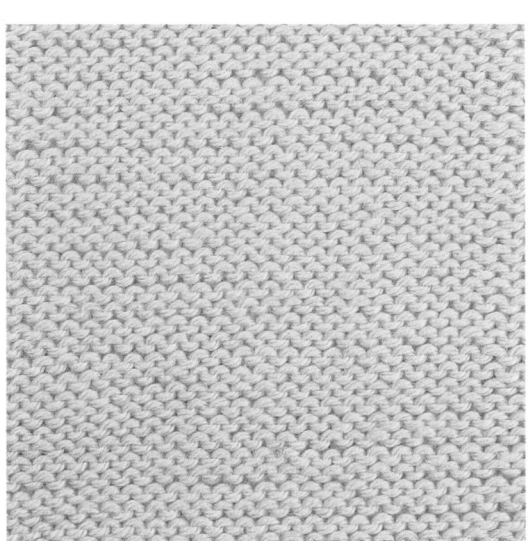

Reverse Stockinette Stitch
Row 1 (right side row): Purl all stitches.
Row 2 (wrong side row): Knit all stitches.
Repeat rows 1 and 2.

Gisela Klöpper

BEAUTIFUL KNITTING PATTERNS

Sterling Publishing Co., Inc.
New York

Translated by Nicole Frank and Daniel Shea
Edited by Hazel Chan

Library of Congress Cataloging-in-Publication Data

Klöpper, Gisela.
 [Schönsten Strickmuster. English]
 Beautiful knitting patterns / Gisela Klöpper.
     p. cm.
 Includes index.
 ISBN 1-4027-0663-4
 1. Knitting—Patterns. 2. Sweaters. I. Title.
TT825.K61513 2003
746.43'20432—dc21

                                   2003005726

10 9 8 7 6 5 4 3 2 1

Published by Sterling Publishing Co., Inc.
387 Park Avenue South, New York, NY 10016
Originally published in Germany by Urania-Ravensburger
under the title *Die Schönsten Strickmuster*
© 2001 by Urania-Ravensburger in the Dornier Medienholding
GmbH, Berlin
English translation © 2003 by Sterling Publishing Co., Inc.
Distributed in Canada by Sterling Publishing
c/o Canadian Manda Group, One Atlantic Avenue, Suite 105
Toronto, Ontario, Canada M6K 3E7
Distributed in Great Britain by Chrysalis Books
64 Brewery Road, London N7 9NT, England
Distributed in Australia by Capricorn Link (Australia) Pty. Ltd.
P.O. Box 704, Windsor, NSW 2756, Australia

Manufactured in China
All rights reserved

Sterling ISBN 1-4027-0663-4

Contents

Preface 5

The History of Knitting 6

Explanations of Knitting Charts and Patterns 8

Variations of Knit and Purl Stitch Patterns 13

Rib Patterns 31

Brioche Stitch Patterns 36

Cable Patterns 45

Lace Patterns 52

Openwork Patterns 63

Jacquard Patterns 71

Minipatterns 82

Slip-Stitch Patterns 87

Knitting into Stitches Below Patterns 94

Patterns from the Alpine Region 99

Aran Isle Patterns 105

Lace Trimming and Patchwork Patterns 113

Various Techniques 121

Index 127

Conversion Tables 128

For my parents,
who handed down to me
the joy of knitting.

Do you like to knit? Then you can identify with the creativity and relaxation of this craft whose tradition is more than one thousand years old.

Knitting has always meant more than simply producing warm clothes. There has been a certain artistry involved. In the early centuries, when more men knitted than women, knitters began creating patterns as shortcuts for their work. As a result, a vast library of patterns grew. Today, the multicolored patterns of the Norwegians and the intricate patterns of the Irish Aran Islands are famous throughout the world.

Today, knitting is as popular as ever: more men and women are discovering it as a relaxing and creative activity for these ever-more stressful times. A virtually inexhaustible selection of yarns and colors helps add to the joy of this handicraft.

In this volume, I have collected more than 250 old and new knitting patterns with which you can make your own project ideas come true. There are, among others, patterns of knit and purl combinations that are simple to make and yet have an intriguing effect. Also included are rib, lace, cable, and jacquard patterns. From all the patterns in this book, you will certainly find the right one for any occasion. No matter whether you are an experienced knitter, or have just recently started knitting again, you will, with the help of these clear knitting charts, patterns, and instructions, create beautiful patterns in each design.

This extensive collection of patterns could only have been made possible with a team that has helped me over many months. Therefore, special thanks go to the coworkers of the company of Coats, Salach, and here particularly to Brigitte Dangelmaier, Frieda Lesle, and Brigitte Schwarz who diligently created samples, as well as all the other helpers who have participated in this project and provided me with much support and encouragement.

I wish you, my fellow knitters, much joy in selecting your favorite patterns. I hope they provide you with great ideas for your own creations and great success with your knitting.

Yours,
Gisela Klöpper

↑
Knitting Sample

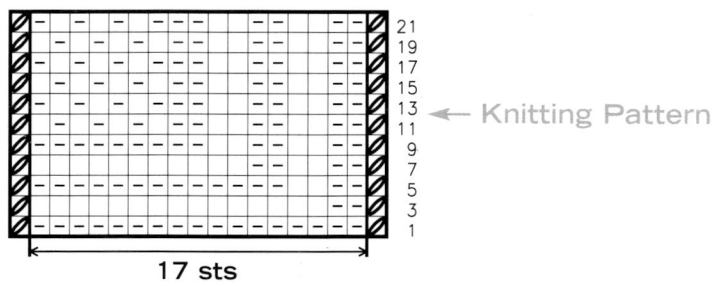

← Knitting Pattern

17 sts

Multiple of 17 sts + 2 edge sts.

On the right side rows, work according to the knitting chart, following the edge stitch and repeat the pattern of 17 stitches. On the wrong side rows, work stitches in pattern. Repeat rows 1–22.

↑
Description

Little is known about the origin of knitting. We can only speculate, since knitted textiles and records have decayed over time. There are, however, written records that give us some hints to specific knitting techniques. For instance, spinning, coloring, and weaving have been hinted at in the songs of heroes of the *Iliad* and the *Odyssey* that arose in the 8th century B.C.E. on clay tablets. There have also been connections made to these techniques on wall paintings in Egyptian tomb chambers.

Textiles have been found that, upon first glance, seem to have been knitted. However, examinations later revealed that they had been worked in related techniques known as "Sprang" (a type of plaiting technique worked on a loom) or "Nalbindung" (loops which have been created and linked to each other with a sewing needle).

The word "knitting" did not exist in either the Ancient Greek or the Latin language. It first appeared in a grammar book that was published in 1530. The word is probably derived from the Old English "cnyttan," which means "to tie with a knot, bind, fasten." It is assumed that Arabic nomads were the first people to knit, and they brought this skill to Egypt. The technique came to Spain via the Moors, who ruled Spain for a long period beginning in 711.

Knitted silk gloves are the first indication of knitting in Europe, since Pope Innocent IV was buried in 1254 with them. Its intricate workmanship indicate that knitting must have already been known long before this date. In the 14th century, knitting seemed to have already been of such great importance that Meister Bertram (1345–1415) painted a triptych for the altar in Buxtehude portraying Mary knitting a shirt with four needles.

The middle of the 16th century gave rise to a new fashion of knee-long pants. The usually sewn stockings of fabric or leather did not provide a pleasing sight because they did not adjust to the shape of the leg. Thus, the knitted silk stockings from Italy became a welcome innovation for the nobility. They were, in fact, so new and valuable that Henry II of France attracted special attention with them at the wedding of his sister in 1559. (The common people continued to wear the sewn-leg dresses.)

The desire of the nobility for knitted silk stockings became so great that knitting as a profession rose. Not only stockings, but also hats, gloves, shirts, blankets, and rugs were knitted in the Intarsia technique. Soon, knitters, as was common among laborers in the Middle Ages, began to organize themselves into guilds—or what we might call unions.

The oldest known guild of stocking knitters was founded in Paris in 1527. The knitting craftsmanship, which was mainly practiced by men, was subjected to strict guild regulations and production rules. A person could only become a master after several years of apprenticeship and after he had knitted several masterpieces within a certain period of

time. One of the masterpieces may have included rugs, as rug were of great importance from approximately 1600 on. The knitted rugs were the size of a 4-foot square (1.20 m) up to about 7 to 10.5 feet (2.20 to 3.20 m).

In 1598, the Englishman William Lee invented the knitting machine, which was the foundation for the stocking production. The stocking, however, could only be knitted flat on the knitting machine and then sewn together later. At first, there was great resistance to Lee's invention because hand knitters feared it would threaten their livelihood. It took some decades before the English finally adapted to it. As a result, England's production of

knitted silk stockings rapidly increased and England became Eurpe's leading producer. In 1656, Jean Claude Hindret, on behalf of French statesman Jean-Baptiste Colbert, explored the production of knitting machines in France and helped it to develop there. Knitting machines began to spread to Germany when Louis XIV revoked the Edict of Nantes in 1685, which had previously granted religious liberty and security to Calvinists, called Huguenots, in France. After the revocation, many Huguenots, many of whom were stocking knitters, left France for Germany in order to practice their faith. In Thuringia, Duke Wilhelm Ernst zu Sachsen-Weimar had the first knitting machines set up. Shortly afterwards several centers of industrial stocking knitting developed in Germany.

With the beginning of industrialization (approximately from the beginning of the 19th century on), the importance of handcrafted knitting decreased. More and more pieces of clothing could be produced much faster and at a much lower price with machines. People, however, continued to knit for their personal needs and pleasures. Thus, handcrafts became a popular occupation of the middle-class woman in the Biedermeier period (about 1800–1850). During this time, many knitting patterns were developed, in particular lace patterns where beads were incorporated into the knitting for things such as bonnets and insets. Knitting became an important part in the education of young women, who were raised to become economical and domestic wives in their future home. As part of their education, girls had to learn how to knit stockings by the age of five. It was only until recently that handcrafts were a required part of home economics in school.

Nowadays, the value of knitting has changed. Knitting is no longer seen as a needed skill but as a creative leisure activity. Today, there is an endless variety of different yarns—from natural materials, such as alpaca and angora, to glittery synthetics made of rayon or acrylic. These different materials, along with the treasure of different stitch patterns in this book, can help you create the most beautiful and one-of-a-kind sweaters, scarves, hats, blankets, and pillows.

Explanation of Knitting Charts and Patterns

The edge stitches are included in most of the patterns, except where the panels are not repeated. The right side rows are read from right to left and the wrong side rows are read from left to right.

If only the right side rows are indicated in the knitting charts, the stitches on wrong side rows are worked in pattern. Exceptions are mentioned in the description of the patterns and in the explanation of the symbols. In the description of the patterns, you also find additional needed information.

If the wrong side rows are shown, then the stitches are each presented in such a way that they appear in the front. For example, a knit stitch is represented on right and wrong side rows by a small empty box. The stitch is, however, knitted on right side rows and purled on wrong side rows. The course of the pattern will become apparent from the chart.

Sts = Stitches.

↤⟶ = Panel where all the rows of the chart are repeated.

The arrows indicate the knitting direction:
← = Right side row.
→ = Wrong side row.

▨ = Selvage or edge stitch.

▣ = No stitch. This is to provide a better overview and is ignored when knitting.

⊞ = Knit 1 garter stitch on right and wrong side rows.

□ = On right side rows, knit 1 stitch. On wrong side rows, purl 1 stitch.

⊟ = On right side rows, purl 1 stitch. On wrong side rows, knit 1 stitch.

◈ = On right side rows, knit into back of stitch. On wrong side rows, purl in back of stitch.

◈ = Make 1 twisted knit stitch (knit into back of stitch) with knitted-in bead.

Ⅴ = On right side rows, knit into back of stitch from the running thread. On wrong side rows, purl into back of stitch from the running thread.

● = Make 1 bobble: Work 5 stitches in 1 stitch (1 knit stitch, 1 yarn over alternately). Only with these 5 stitches, knit 4 rows in stockinette stitch and, counting from tip of the needle, pass stitches 2–5 over stitch 1.

○ = Make 1 yarn over, then purl the yarn over in the following wrong side row.

φ = Make 1 yarn over, purl 1 stitch and then knit 1 stitch from the yarn over in the following row.

○○ = Make 2 yarn overs, purl 1 stitch and knit 1 stitch from the yarn overs in the following row.

② = On right side rows, knit 2 stitches together. On the wrong side rows, purl 2 stitches together.

ƨ = Work a single decrease slanting to the left by passing 1 stitch over the other: Slip 1 stitch knitwise, knit the following stitch and then pass the slipped stitch over the knitted stitch, or purl into the back of 2 stitches on wrong side rows.

②̲ = On right side rows, purl 2 stitches together. On wrong side rows, knit 2 stitches together.

③ = On right side rows, knit 3 stitches together, On wrong side rows, purl 3 stitches together.

③̲ = On right side rows, purl 3 stitches together. On wrong side rows, knit 3 stitches together.

⊡ = Work a double decrease slanting to the right: Slip 1 stitch knitwise, then knit the 2 following stitches together and pass the slipped stitch over the 2 knitted together stitches.

⊼ = On right side rows, slip 2 stitches together knitwise, knit the following stitch and pass the two slipped stitches over it.

⌒ = Cast off 1 stitch.

⊓ = On right side rows, slip 1 stitch purlwise with yarn in back of work. On wrong side rows, slip 1 stitch purlwise with yarn in front of work.

⊓ = On right side rows, slip 1 stitch purlwise with yarn in front of work. On wrong side rows, slip 1 stitch purlwise with yarn in back of work.

← ⊓ = On right side rows, slip 1 stitch purlwise with yarn in back of work, knit 2 stitches and pass slipped stitch over.

← ⊓ = On right side rows, slip 1 stitch purlwise with yarn in back of work, knit 3 stitches and pass slipped stitch over.

⊓ → = On wrong side rows, slip 1 stitch purlwise with yarn in front of work, purl 3 stitches and pass slipped stitch over.

← ○ = On right side rows, make 1 yarn over, knit 2 stitches and pass the yarn over over the 2 knit stitches.

◉ = On right side rows, make 1 yarn over, then knit the following stitch. On wrong side rows, make 1 yarn over, then purl the following stitch. On the following row, drop the yarn over and knit the stitch on right side rows; purl respectively on wrong side rows.

Ⅾ = On right side rows, make 2 yarn overs, then knit the following stitch. On wrong side rows, 2 yarn overs, then purl the following stitch. On the following row, drop the yarn overs and knit the stitch on right side rows; purl respectively on wrong side rows.

⊗ = On right side rows, make 3 yarn overs on right side rows, then knit the following stitch. On wrong side rows, make 3 yarn overs, then purl the following stitch. On the following row, drop the yarn overs.

↓ = Drop the yarn over off the needle.

⋒ = Slip stitch only purlwise and drop yarn overs; the stitch is not knitted.

♠◇ = Slip 2 stitches purlwise (yarn in back of work), dropping the yarn overs and stretching the stitches. Afterwards, lift the stitches back onto the left-hand needle and, from both stitches, knit into back of 1 stitch and purl into back of the other one by inserting needle into both stitches. Then slip the stitches off the left-hand needle.

♠◇♦◇ = Slip 4 stitches purlwise (yarn in back of work), dropping the yarn overs and stretching the stitches. Afterwards, lift the stitches back onto the left-hand needle and, from the 4 stitches, knit into back of 1 stitch and purl into back of the other. Repeat knitting into back of 1 stitch and purling into back of the other. Knit 4 stitches in total by inserting needle into all stitches. Then slip the stitches off the left-hand needle.

Explanation of Knitting Charts and Patterns

◇◆◇◆◇ = Slip 5 stitches purlwise (yarn in back of work), dropping the yarn overs and stretching the stitches. Afterwards, lift the stitches back onto the left-hand needle and, from the 5 stitches, knit into back of 1 stitch and purl into back of the other. Once more, knit into back of 1 stitch and purl into back of the other and knit into back of stitch. Knit 5 stitches in total by inserting needle into all stitches. Then slip the stitches off the left-hand needle.

⌐ = Take up the floats (threads that are carried on the wrong side) with the left-hand needle and, by entering from top to bottom, insert needle in the back of the threads, then work the threads together with the stitch by twisting them.

Ʊ = Slip 1 stitch with 1 yarn over purlwise.

▲ = On right or wrong side rows, knit stitch and yarn over together.

△ = On right or wrong side rows, purl stitch and yarn over together.

Ʊ = On wrong side rows, slip 1 stitch with 1 yarn over purlwise. On right side rows, knit stitch and yarn over together.

☰ = On right side rows, slip 1 stitch with 1 yarn over purlwise. On wrong side rows, knit stitch and yarn over together.

I = On right side rows, knit 1 stitch. On wrong side rows, slip stitch with 1 yarn over purlwise.

Ꝺ = On right side rows, knit the brioche stitch (including the yarn over) and the previous stitch together. On wrong side rows, slip stitch with 1 yarn over purlwise.

Ꝺ = On right side rows, slip brioche stitch (including the yarn over) knitwise, then knit the following stitch and pass the slipped stitch (including the yarn over) over. On wrong side rows, slip stitch with 1 yarn over purlwise.

◺ = On a cable needle, hold 1 stitch in front of work, knit 1 stitch, then knit the stitch from the cable needle.

◹ = On a cable needle, hold 1 stitch in back of work, knit 1 stitch, then knit the stitch from the cable needle.

◺ = On a cable needle, hold 1 stitch in front of work, purl 1 stitch, then knit the stitch from the cable needle.

◹ = On a cable needle, hold 1 stitch in back of work, knit 1 stitch, then purl the stitch from the cable needle.

2◺1 = On a cable needle, hold 2 stitches in front of work, knit 1 stitch, then knit the stitches from the cable needle.

1◹2 = On a cable needle, hold 1 stitch in back of work, knit 2 stitches, then knit the stitch from the cable needle.

1◺2 = On a cable needle, hold 1 stitch in front of work, knit 2 stitches, then knit the stitch from the cable needle.

2◹1 = On a cable needle, hold 2 stitches in back of work, knit 1 stitch, then knit the stitches from the cable needle.

2◺1 = On a cable needle, hold 2 stitches in front of work, purl 1 stitch, then knit the stitches from the cable needle.

-◹2 = On a cable needle, hold 1 stitch in back of work, knit 2 stitches, then purl the stitches from the cable needle.

`[2 / 2]` = On a cable needle, hold 2 stitches in front of work, knit 2 stitches, then knit the stitches from the cable needle.

`[2 \ 2]` = On a cable needle, hold 2 stitches in back of work, knit 2 stitches, then knit the stitches from the cable needle.

`[2 / -]` = On a cable needle, hold 2 stitches in front of work, purl 2 stitches, then knit the stitches from the cable needle.

`[- - / 2]` = On a cable needle, hold 2 stitches in back of work, knit 2 stitches, then purl the stitches from the cable needle.

`[2 / - -]` = On a cable needle, hold 2 stitches in front of work, purl 3 stitches, then knit the stitches from the cable needle.

`[- - - / 2]` = On a cable needle, hold 3 stitches in back of work, knit 2 stitches, then purl the stitches from the cable needle.

`[2 - / 2]` = On a cable needle, hold 2 stitches in front of work, knit 2 stitches and purl 1 stitch, then knit the stitches from the cable needle.

`[2 - / 2]` = On a cable needle, hold 3 stitches in back of work, knit 2 stitches, then, from the cable needle, purl 1 stitch and knit 2 stitches.

`[2 - - / 2]` = On a cable needle, hold 2 stitches in front of work, knit 2 stitches and purl 2 stitches, then knit the stitches from the cable needle.

`[2 - - / 2]` = On a cable needle, hold 4 stitches in back of work, knit 2 stitches, then, from the cable needle, purl 2 stitches and knit 2 stitches.

`[3 / 3]` = On a cable needle, hold 3 stitches in front of work, knit 3 stitches, then knit the stitches from the cable needle.

`[3 \ 3]` = On a cable needle, hold 3 stitches in back of work, knit 3 stitches, then knit the stitches from the cable needle.

`[3 / - -]` = On a cable needle, hold 3 stitches in front of work, purl 2 stitches, then knit the stitches from the cable needle.

`[- - / 3]` = On a cable needle, hold 2 stitches in back of work, knit 3 stitches, then purl the stitches from the cable needle.

`[3 / - - -]` = On a cable needle, hold 3 stitches in front of work, purl 3 stitches, then knit the stitches from the cable needle.

`[- - - / 3]` = On a cable needle, hold 3 stitches in back of work, knit 3 stitches, then purl the stitches from the cable needle.

`[3 / 1]` = On a cable needle, hold 3 stitches in front of work, knit 1 stitch, then knit the stitches from the cable needle.

`[1 / 3]` = On a cable needle, hold 1 stitch in back of work, knit 3 stitches, then knit the stitch from the cable needle.

`[3 \ -]` = On a cable needle, hold 3 stitches in front of work, purl 1 stitch, then knit the stitches from the cable needle.

`[- / 3]` = On a cable needle, hold 1 stitch in back of work, knit 3 stitches, then purl the stitch of the cable needle.

`[4 / 4]` = On a cable needle, hold 4 stitches in front of work, knit 4 stitches, then knit the stitches from the cable needle.

= On a cable needle, hold 4 stitches in back of work, knit 4 stitches, then knit the stitches from the cable needle.

= On a cable needle, hold 4 stitches in front of work, purl 4 stitches, then knit the stitches from the cable needle.

= On a cable needle, hold 4 stitches in back of work, knit 4 stitches, then purl the stitches from the cable needle.

= On right side rows, hold 1 stitch on a cable needle in front of work, knit into back of stitch, then knit into back of the cable needle stitch. On wrong side rows, hold 1 stitch on a cable needle in front of work, purl into back of stitch, then purl into back of the cable needle stitch.

= On right side rows, hold 1 stitch on a cable needle in back of work, knit into back of stitch, then knit into back of the cable needle stitch. On wrong side rows, hold 1 stitch on a cable needle in back of work, purl into back of stitch, then purl into back of the cable needle stitch.

= On right side rows, hold 1 stitch on a cable needle in front of work, purl 1 stitch, then knit into back of the cable needle stitch. On wrong side rows, hold 1 stitch on a cable needle in front of work, purl into back of stitch, then knit the cable needle stitch.

= On right side rows, hold 1 stitch on a cable needle in back of work, knit into back of stitch, then purl the stitch of the cable needle. On wrong side rows, hold 1 stitch on a cable needle in back of work, knit 1 stitch, then purl into back of the cable needle stitch.

= On right side rows, hold 2 stitches on a cable needle in front of work, knit into back of stitch, then knit into back of the cable needle stitches. On wrong side rows, hold 1 stitch on a cable needle in front of work, purl 2 stitches, then purl into back of cable needle stitch.

= On right side rows, hold 1 stitch on a cable needle in back of work, knit into back of 2 stitches, then knit into back of the cable needle stitch. On wrong side rows, hold 2 stitches on a cable needle in back of work, purl into back of stitch, then purl the stitches from the cable needle.

= On right side rows, hold 2 stitches on a cable needle in back of work, knit into back of stitch, then knit into back of the cable needle stitches.

= On right side rows, hold 2 stitches on a cable needle in front of work, purl 1 stitch, then knit into back of the cable needle stitches. On wrong side rows, hold 1 stitch on a cable needle in front of work, purl into back of 2 stitches, then knit the stitch from the cable needle.

= On right side rows, hold 1 stitch on a cable needle in back of work, knit into back of 2 stitches, then purl the stitch of the cable needle. On wrong side rows, hold 2 stitches on a cable needle in back of work, knit 1 stitch, then purl into back of cable needle stitches.

= On right side rows, hold 2 stitches on a cable needle in front of work, knit into back of 2 stitches, then knit into back of the cable needle stitches.

= On right side rows, hold 2 stitches on a cable needle in back of work, knit into back of 2 stitches, then knit into back of the cable needle stitches.

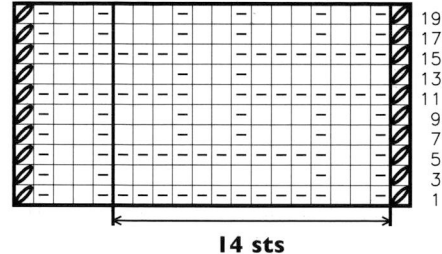

14 sts

Multiple of 14 sts + 4 + 2 edge sts

On right side rows, work according to the knitting chart. Repeat the pattern of 14 stitches following the edge stitch and end as drawn. On wrong side rows, work stitches in pattern. Repeat rows 1–20.

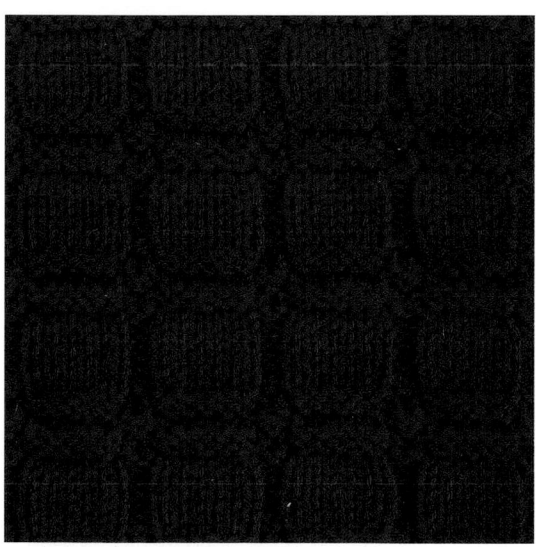

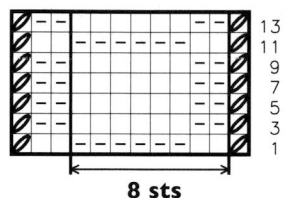

8 sts

Multiple of 8 sts + 2 + 2 edge sts

On right side rows, work according to the knitting chart. Repeat the pattern of 8 stitches following the edge stitch and end as drawn. On wrong side rows, work stitches in pattern. Repeat rows 1–14.

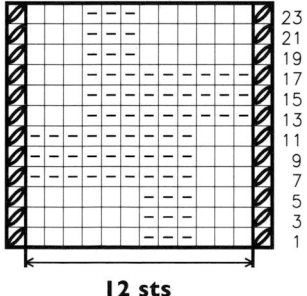

12 sts

Multiple of 12 sts + 2 edge sts

On right side rows, work according to the knitting chart. Repeat the pattern of 12 stitches following the edge stitch. On wrong side rows, purl all stitches. Repeat rows 1–24.

Variations of Knit and Purl Stitch Patterns

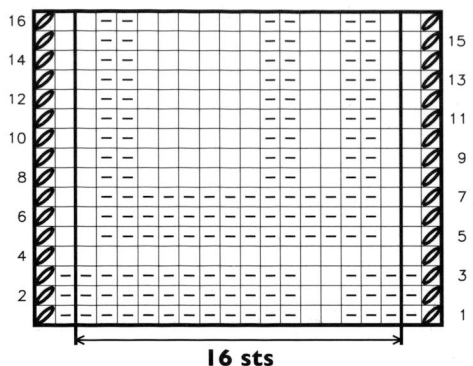

16 sts

Multiple of 16 sts + 2 + 2 edge sts

On right and wrong side rows, work according to the knitting chart. Following the edge stitch, begin as indicated in the chart. Repeat the pattern of 16 stitches and end as drawn. Repeat rows 1–16.

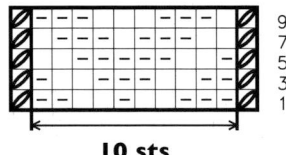

10 sts

Multiple of 10 sts + 2 edge sts

On right side rows, work according to the knitting chart. Repeat the pattern of 10 stitches following the edge stitch. On wrong side rows, purl all stitches. Repeat rows 1–10.

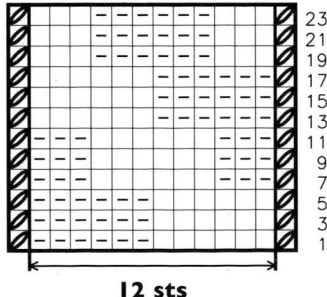

12 sts

Multiple of 12 sts + 2 edge sts

On right side rows, work according to the knitting chart. Repeat the pattern of 12 stitches following the edge stitch. On wrong side rows, purl all stitches. Repeat rows 1–24.

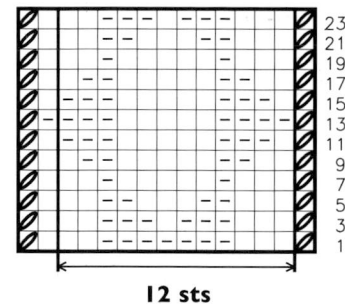

Multiple of 12 sts + 1 + 2 edge sts

On right side rows, work according to the knitting chart. Repeat the pattern of 12 stitches following the edge stitch and end as drawn. On wrong side rows, purl all stitches. Repeat rows 1–24.

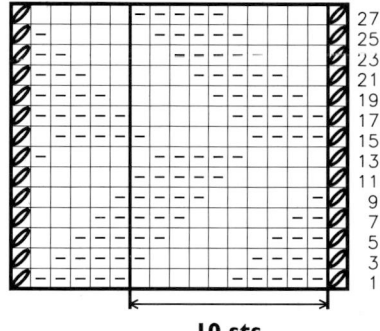

Multiple of 10 sts + 5 sts + 2 edge sts

On right side rows, work according to the knitting chart. Repeat the pattern of 10 stitches following the edge stitch and end as drawn. On wrong side rows, purl all stitches. Repeat rows 1–28.

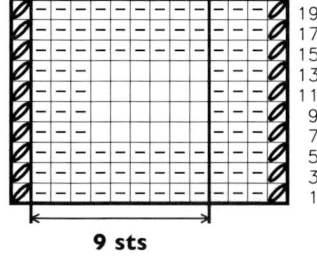

Multiple of 9 sts + 3 sts + 2 edge sts

On right side rows, work according to the knitting chart. Repeat the pattern of 9 stitches following the edge stitch and end as drawn. On wrong side rows, purl all stitches. Repeat rows 1–20.

Variations of Knit and Purl Stitch Patterns

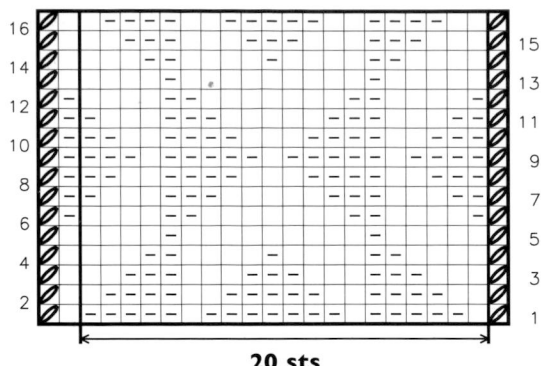

Multiple of 20 sts + 1 + 2 edge sts

On right and wrong side rows, work according to the knitting chart. Beginning as indicated in the chart, repeat the pattern of 20 stitches and end as drawn. Repeat rows 1–16.

20 sts

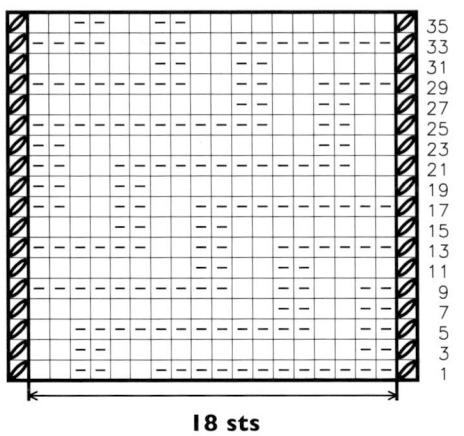

18 sts

Multiple of 18 sts + 2 edge sts

On right side rows, work according to the knitting chart. Following the edge stitch, repeat the pattern of 18 stitches and then edge stitch. On wrong side rows, work stitches in pattern. Repeat rows 1–36.

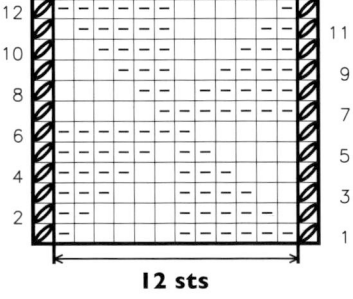

12 sts

Multiple of 12 sts + 2 edge sts

On right and wrong side rows, work according to the knitting chart. Following the edge stitch, repeat the pattern of 12 stitches and then edge stitch. Repeat rows 1–12.

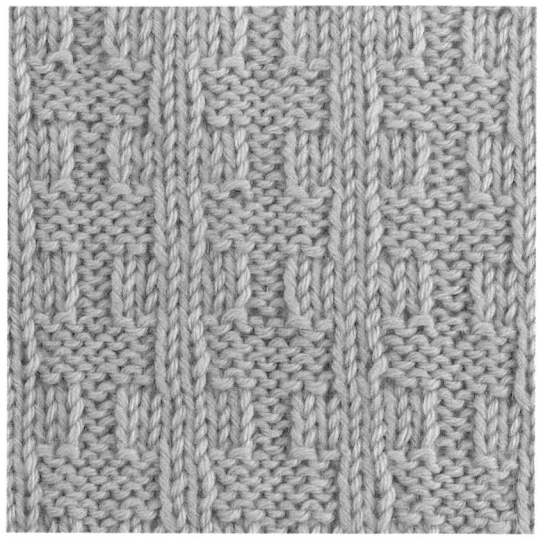

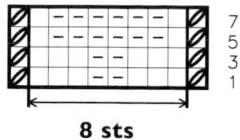

8 sts

Multiple of 8 sts + 2 edge sts

On right side rows, work according to the knitting chart. Following the edge stitch, repeat the pattern of 8 stitches and then edge stitch. On wrong side rows, work stitches in pattern. Repeat rows 1–8.

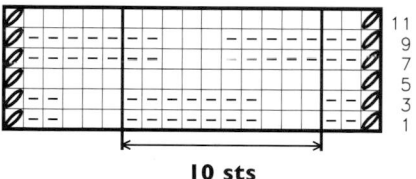

10 sts

Multiple of 10 sts + 7 + 2 edge sts

On right side rows, work according to the knitting chart. Following the edge stitch, begin as indicated in the chart. Repeat the pattern of 10 stitches and end as drawn. On wrong side rows, work stitches in pattern. Repeat rows 1–12.

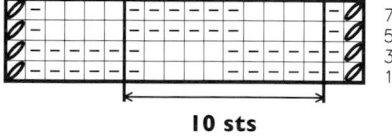

10 sts

Multiple of 10 sts + 6 + 2 edge sts

On right side rows, work according to the knitting chart. Beginning as indicated in the chart, repeat the pattern of 10 stitches and end as drawn. On wrong side rows, work stitches in pattern. Repeat rows 1–8.

Variations of Knit and Purl Stitch Patterns

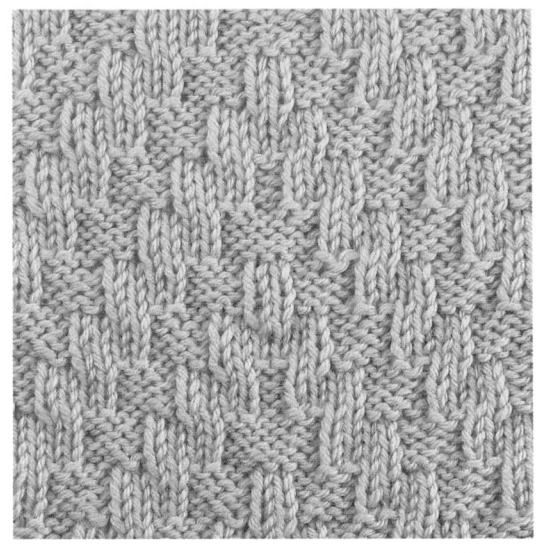

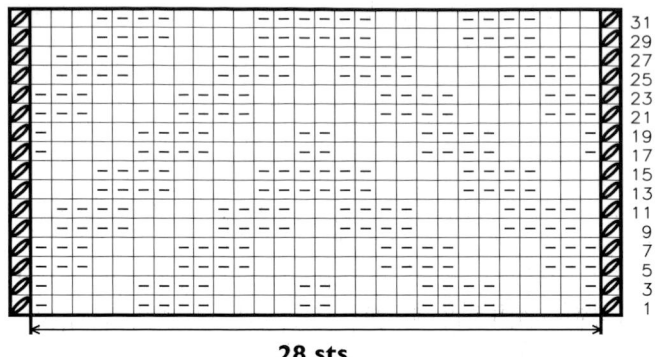

28 sts

Multiple of 28 sts + 2 edge sts

On right side rows, work according to the knitting chart. Following the edge stitch, repeat the pattern of 28 stitches and then edge stitch. On wrong side rows, work stitches in pattern. Repeat rows 1–32.

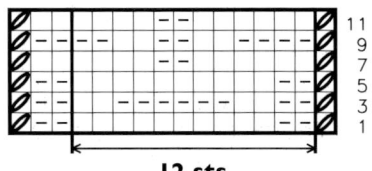

12 sts

Multiple of 12 sts + 2 + 2 edge sts

On right side rows, work according to the knitting chart. Following the edge stitch, repeat the pattern of 12 stitches to edge stitch and end as drawn. On wrong side rows, work stitches in pattern. Repeat rows 1–12.

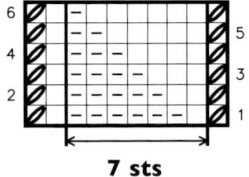

7 sts

Multiple of 7 sts + 1 + 2 edge sts

On right and wrong side rows, work according to the knitting chart. Following the edge stitch, repeat the pattern of 7 stitches to edge stitch and end as drawn. Repeat rows 1–6.

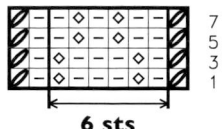

Multiple of 6 sts + 1 + 2 edge sts

On right side rows, work according to the knitting chart. Repeat the pattern of 6 stitches following the edge stitch and end as drawn. On wrong side rows, work stitches in pattern. Note: Knit into the back of stitches on right side rows and purl into the back of stitches on wrong side rows. Repeat rows 1–8.

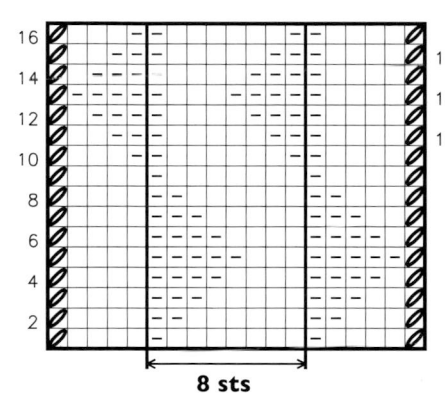

Multiple of 8 sts + 1 + 2 edge sts

On right and wrong side rows, work according to the knitting chart. Beginning as indicated in the chart, repeat the pattern of 8 stitches and end as drawn. Repeat rows 1–16.

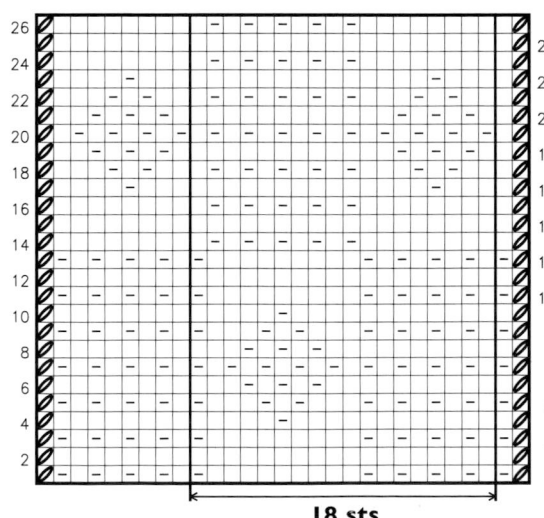

Multiple of 18 sts + 9 + 2 edge sts

On right and wrong side rows, work according to the knitting chart. Beginning as indicated in the chart, repeat the pattern of 18 stitches and end as drawn. Repeat rows 1–26.

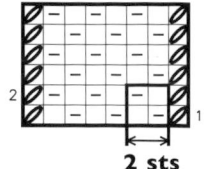

2 sts

Even number of stitches

On right and wrong side rows, work according to the knitting chart. Repeat the pattern of 2 stitches following the edge stitch. Repeat rows 1 and 2.

If you knit this pattern with several colors, you will obtain a tweed effect. For this sample swatch, knit 1 row each in dark green, medium green, and light green, and then repeat these 3 rows. Knit in rows with a circular needle and, following each row, slide the stitches with the necessary yarn at the end of the needle.

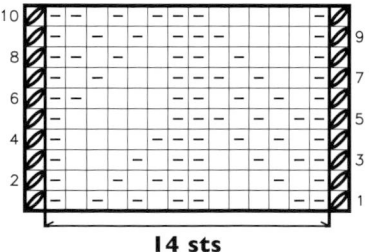

14 sts

Multiple of 14 sts + 2 edge sts

On right and wrong side rows, work according to the knitting chart. Following the edge stitch, repeat the pattern of 14 stitches and then edge stitch. Repeat rows 1–10.

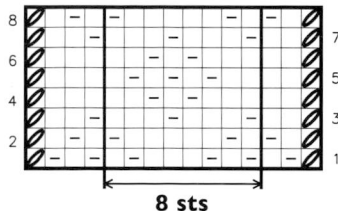

8 sts

Multiple of 8 sts + 5 + 2 edge sts

On right and wrong side rows, work according to the knitting chart. Beginning as indicated in the chart, repeat the pattern of 8 stitches and end as drawn. Repeat rows 1–8.

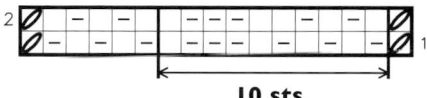

10 sts

Multiple of 10 sts + 5 + 2 edge sts

On right and wrong side rows, work according to the knitting chart. Repeat the pattern of 10 stitches and end as drawn. Repeat rows 1 and 2.

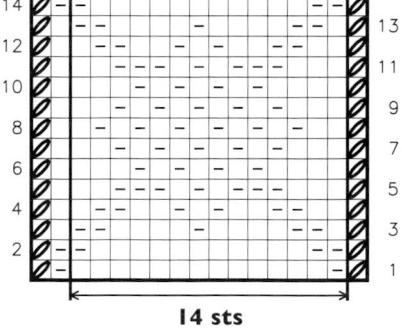

14 sts

Multiple of 14 sts + 1 + 2 edge sts

On right and wrong side rows, work according to the knitting chart. Following the edge stitch, repeat the pattern of 14 stitches and end as drawn. Repeat rows 1–14.

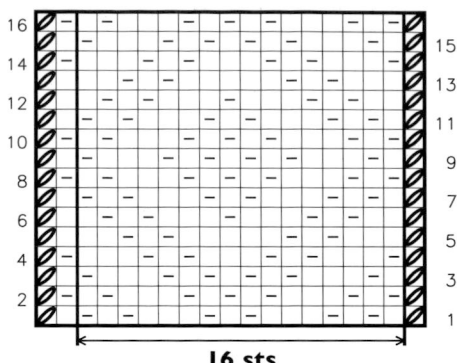

16 sts

Multiple of 16 sts + 1 + 2 edge sts

On right and wrong side rows, work according to the knitting chart. Repeat the pattern of 16 stitches and end as drawn. Repeat rows 1–16.

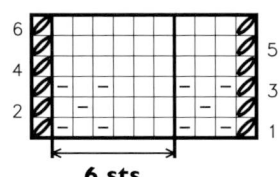

6 sts

Multiple of 6 sts + 3 + 2 edge sts

On right and wrong side rows, work according to the knitting chart. Begin as indicated in the chart and repeat the pattern of 6 stitches and then edge stitch. Repeat rows 1–6.

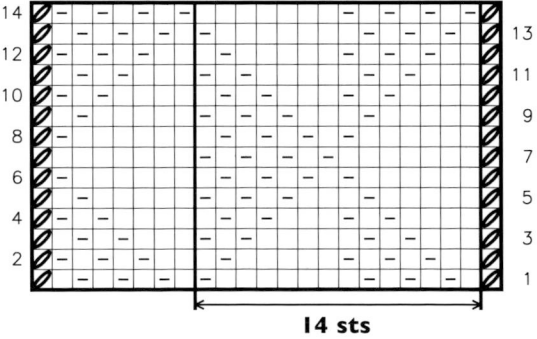

14 sts

Multiple of 14 sts + 7 + 2 edge sts

On right and wrong side rows, work according to the knitting chart. Repeat the pattern of 14 stitches and end as drawn. Repeat rows 1–14.

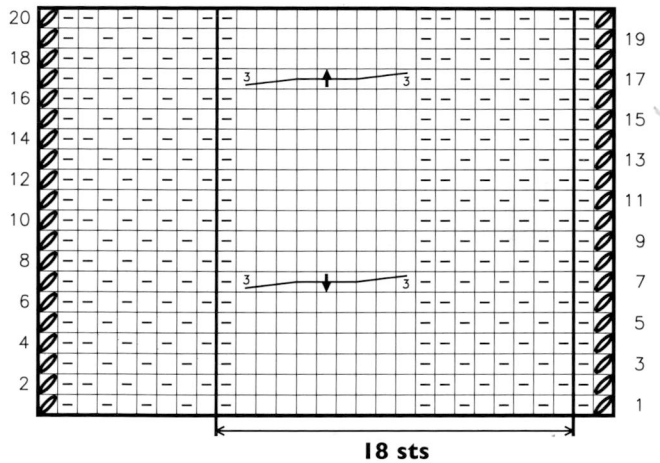

Panel of 18 sts + 9 + 2 edge sts

On right and wrong side rows, work according to the knitting chart. Beginning as indicated in the chart, repeat the pattern of 18 stitches and end as drawn. Repeat rows 1–20.

= Hold 3 stitches on the 1st cable needle in back of work and 3 stitches on the 2nd cable needle in front of work. Knit 3 stitches, knit stitches from the 2nd cable needle and then knit stitches from the 1st cable needle.

= Hold 3 stitches on the 1st cable needle in back of work, hold 3 stitches on the 2nd cable needle in back of the 1st cable needle. Knit 3 stitches, knit stitches from 2nd cable needle and then knit stitches from 1st cable needle.

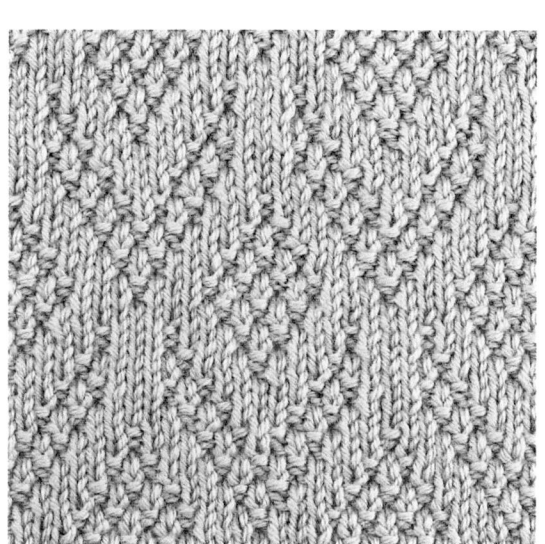

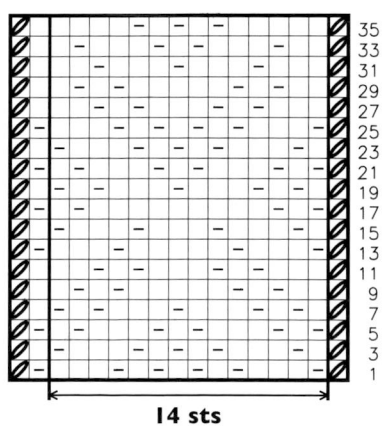

Multiple of 14 sts + 1 + 2 edge sts

On right side rows, work according to the knitting chart. Repeat the pattern of 14 stitches, following the edge stitch and end as drawn. On wrong side rows, work stitches in pattern. Repeat rows 1–36.

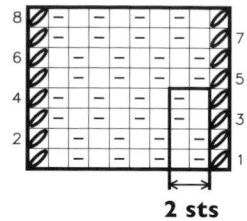

2 sts

Even number of stitches

On right and wrong side rows, work according to the knitting chart. Following the edge stitch, repeat the pattern of 2 stitches and then edge stitch. Repeat rows 1–4.

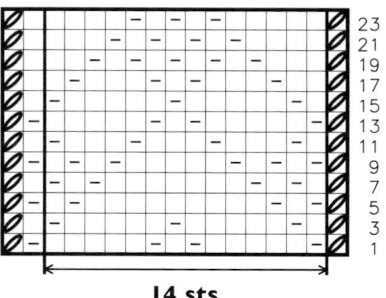

14 sts

Multiple of 14 sts + 1 + 2 edge sts

On right side rows, work according to the knitting chart. Repeat the pattern of 14 stitches and end as drawn. On wrong side rows, work stitches in pattern. Repeat rows 1–24.

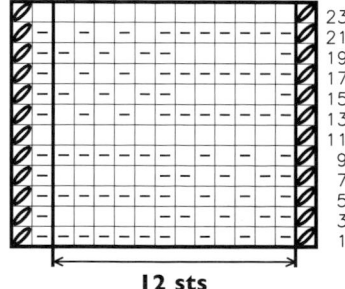

12 sts

Multiple of 12 sts + 1 + 2 edge sts

On right side rows, work according to the knitting chart. Following the edge stitch, repeat the pattern of 12 stitches and end as drawn. On wrong side rows, work stitches in pattern. Repeat rows 1–24.

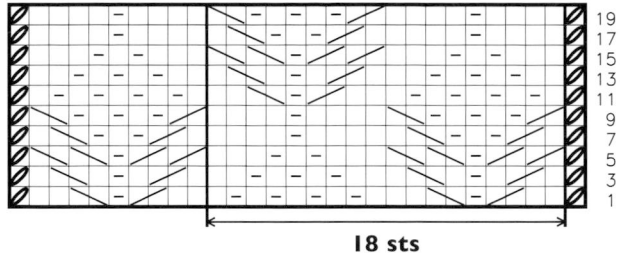

18 sts

Multiple of 18 sts + 9 + 2 edge sts

On right side rows, work according to the knitting chart. Following the edge stitch, repeat the pattern of 18 stitches and end as drawn. On wrong side rows, work stitches in pattern. Repeat rows 1–20.

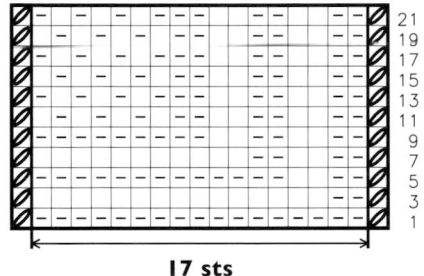

17 sts

Multiple of 17 sts + 2 edge sts

On right side rows, work according to the knitting chart. Repeat the pattern of 17 stitches following the edge stitch. On wrong side rows, work stitches in pattern. Repeat rows 1–22.

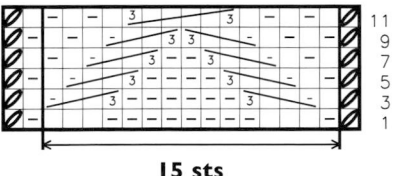

15 sts

Multiple of 15 sts + 1 + 2 edge sts

On right side rows, work according to the knitting chart. Repeat the pattern of 15 stitches following the edge stitch and end as drawn. On wrong side rows, work stitches in pattern. Repeat rows 1–12.

Variations of Knit and Purl Stitch Patterns

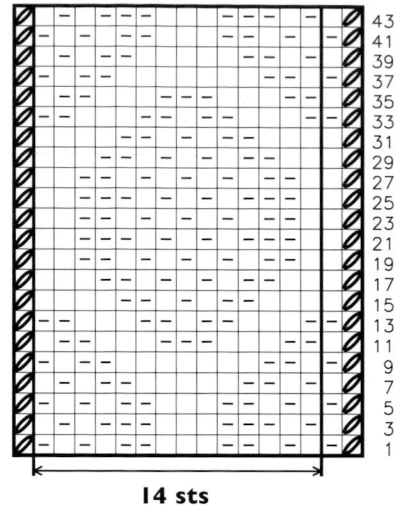

14 sts

Multiple of 14 sts + 1 + 2 edge sts

On right side rows, work according to the knitting chart. Beginning as indicated in the chart, repeat the pattern of 14 stitches and then edge stitch. On wrong side rows, work stitches in pattern. Repeat rows 1–44.

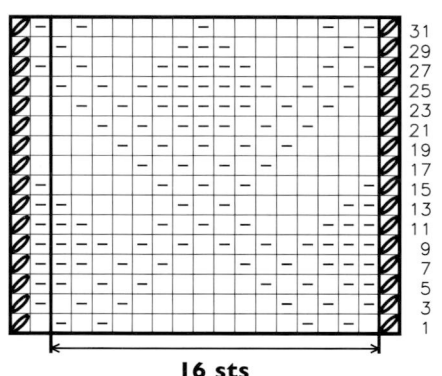

16 sts

Multiple of 16 sts + 1 + 2 edge sts

On right side rows, work according to the knitting chart. Following the edge stitch, repeat the pattern of 16 stitches and end as drawn. On wrong side rows, work stitches in pattern. Repeat rows 1–32.

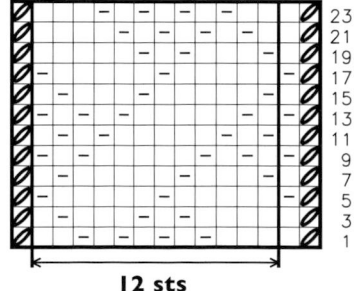

12 sts

Multiple of 12 sts + 1 + 2 edge sts

On right side rows, work according to the knitting chart. Beginning as indicated in the chart, repeat the pattern of 12 stitches and then edge stitch. On wrong side rows, work stitches in pattern. Repeat rows 1–24.

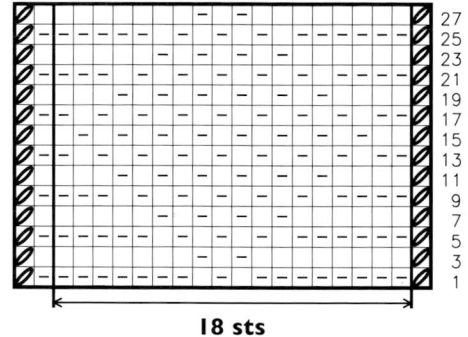

18 sts

Multiple of 18 sts + 1 + 2 edge sts

On right side rows, work according to the knitting chart. Following the edge stitch, repeat the pattern of 18 stitches and end as drawn. On wrong side rows, work stitches in pattern. Repeat rows 1–28.

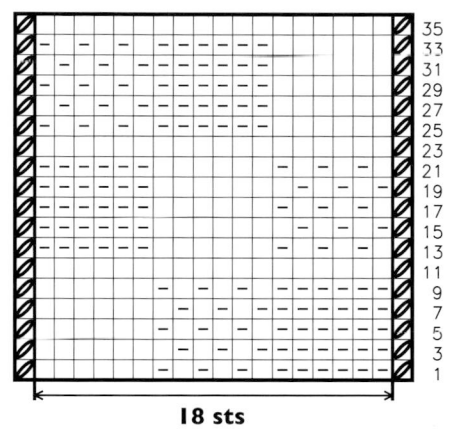

18 sts

Multiple of 18 sts + 2 edge sts

On right side rows, work according to the knitting chart. Repeat the pattern of 18 stitches following the edge stitch. On wrong side rows, work stitches in pattern. Repeat rows 1–36.

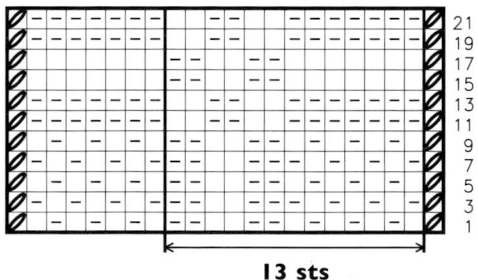

13 sts

Multiple of 13 sts + 7 + 2 edge sts

On right side rows, work according to the knitting chart. Repeat the pattern of 13 stitches following the edge stitch and end as drawn. On wrong side rows, work stitches in pattern. Repeat rows 1–22.

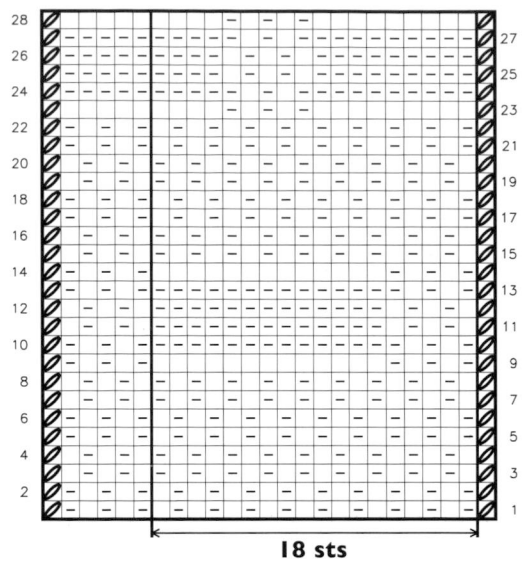

18 sts

Multiple of 18 sts + 5 + 2 edge sts

On right and wrong side rows, work according to the knitting chart. Repeat the pattern of 18 stitches following the edge stitch and end as drawn. Repeat rows 1–28.

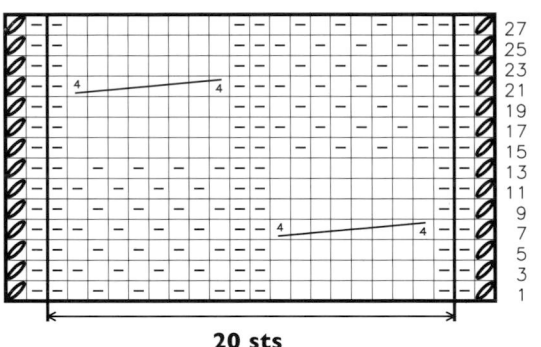

20 sts

Multiple of 20 sts + 2 + 2 edge sts

On right side rows, work according to the knitting chart. Beginning as indicated in the chart, repeat the pattern of 20 stitches and end as drawn. On wrong side rows, work stitches in pattern. Repeat rows 1–28.

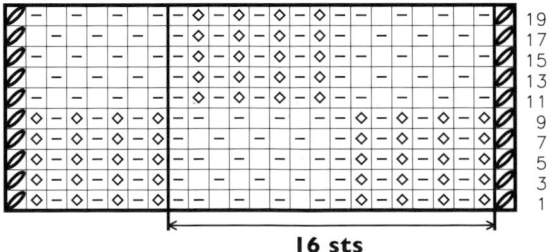

16 sts

Multiple of 16 sts + 7 + 2 edge sts

On right side rows, work according to the knitting chart. Following the edge stitch, repeat the pattern of 16 stitches and end as drawn. On wrong side rows, work stitches in pattern. Note: Knit into the back of stitches on right side rows and purl into the back of stitches on wrong side rows. Repeat rows 1–20.

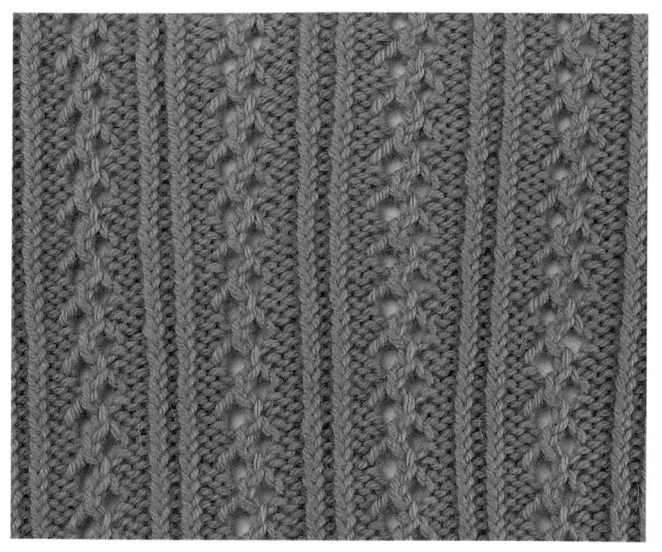

Rib Patterns

When most knitters encounter the term "rib pattern," they usually think of ribbing along the edge of sweaters, jackets, or socks. With vertical ribs of knit and purl stitches—comprised mostly of 1 knit stitch and 1 purl stitch, or 2 knit stitches and 2 purl stitches—you will get an elastic knit pattern that is good for waistbands and cuffs.

Rib patterns can, however, also consist of many other elements, such as cable stitches or lace stitches with knit and purl stitches. You will be surprised by the many variations that can be created.

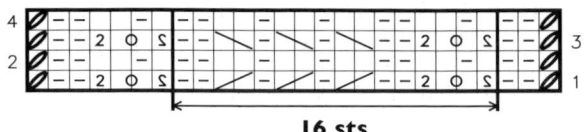

16 sts

Multiple of 16 sts + 8 + 2 edge sts

On right and wrong side rows, work according to knitting chart. Beginning as indicated in the chart, repeat the pattern of 16 stitches and end as drawn. On wrong side rows, purl 1 stitch and knit 1 stitch from yarn over as drawn. Repeat rows 1–4.

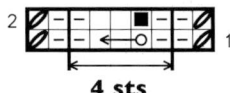

4 sts

Multiple of 4 sts + 2 + 2 edge sts

On right and wrong side rows, work according to knitting chart. Beginning as indicated in the chart, repeat the pattern of 4 stitches and end as drawn. Repeat rows 1 and 2.

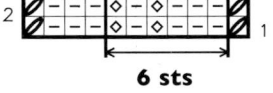

6 sts

Multiple of 6 sts + 3 + 2 edge sts

On right and wrong side rows, work according to knitting chart. Following the edge stitch, repeat the pattern of 6 stitches and end as drawn. Repeat rows 1 and 2.

6 sts

Multiple of 6 sts + 2 edge sts

On right side rows, work according to knitting chart. Beginning as indicated in the chart, repeat the pattern of 6 stitches and end as drawn. On wrong side rows, work stitches in pattern. Repeat rows 1–4.

8 sts

Multiple of 8 sts + 5 + 2 edge sts

On right and wrong side rows, work according to knitting chart. Beginning as indicated in the chart, repeat the pattern of 8 stitches and end as drawn. Repeat rows 1 and 2.

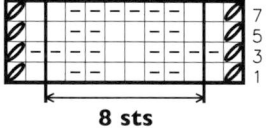

8 sts

Multiple of 8 sts + 2 + 2 edge sts

On right side rows, work according to knitting chart. Beginning as indicated in the chart, repeat the pattern of 8 stitches and end as drawn. On wrong side rows, work stitches in pattern. Repeat rows 1–8.

Rib Patterns

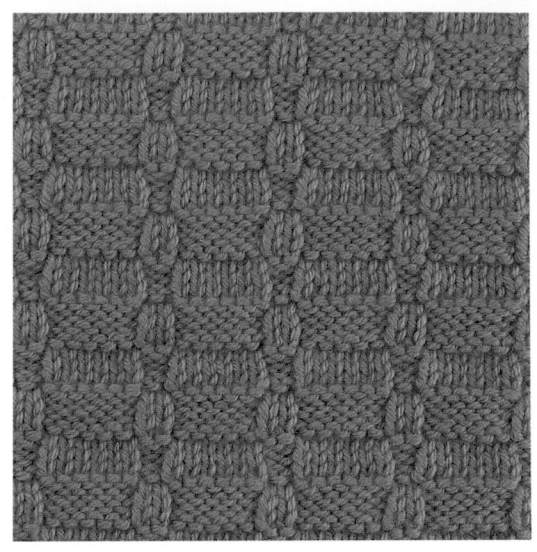

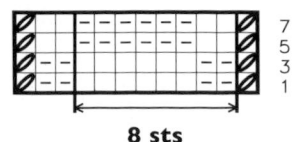

8 sts

Multiple of 8 sts + 2 + 2 edge sts

On right side rows, work according to knitting chart. Following the edge stitch, repeat the pattern of 8 stitches and end as drawn. On wrong side rows, work stitches in pattern. Repeat rows 1–8.

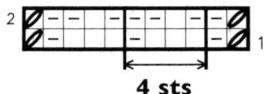

4 sts

Multiple of 4 sts + 1 + 2 edge sts

On right and wrong side rows, work according to knitting chart. Beginning as indicated in the chart, repeat the pattern of 4 stitches and end as drawn. Repeat rows 1 and 2.

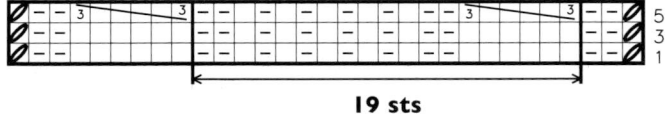

19 sts

Panel of 19 sts + 10 + 2 edge sts

On right side rows, work according to knitting chart. Beginning as indicated in the chart, repeat the pattern of 19 stitches and end as drawn. On wrong side rows, work stitches in pattern. Repeat rows 1–6.

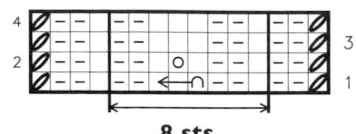

8 sts

Panel of 8 sts + 5 + 2 edge sts

On right and wrong side rows, work according to knitting chart. Beginning as indicated in the chart, repeat the pattern of 8 stitches and end as drawn. Repeat rows 1–4.

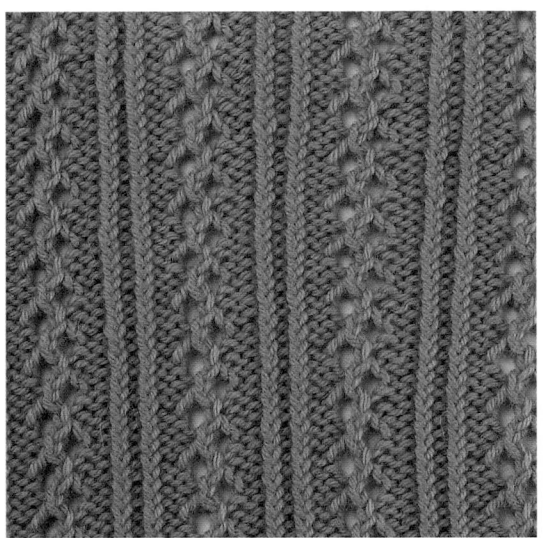

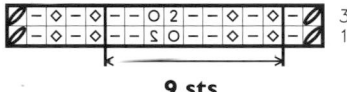

9 sts

Panel of 9 sts + 5 + 2 edge sts

On right side rows, work according to knitting chart. Beginning as indicated in the chart, repeat the pattern of 9 stitches and end as drawn. On wrong side rows, work stitches in pattern. Note: Knit into the back of stitches on right side rows and purl into back of stitches on wrong side rows and purl the yarn overs. Repeat rows 1–4.

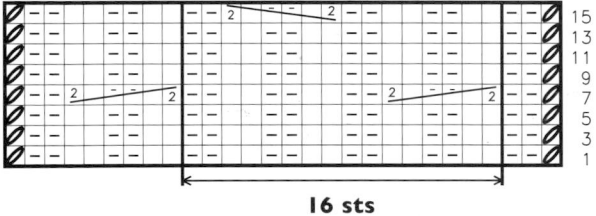

16 sts

Panel of 16 sts + 10 + 2 edge sts

On right side rows, work according to knitting chart. Beginning as indicated in the chart, repeat the pattern of 16 stitches and end as drawn. On wrong side rows, work stitches in pattern. Repeat rows 1–16.

Brioche Stitch Patterns

Brioche stitch patterns produce a very big and soft knit, so they are great for warm sweaters and cozy scarves. Used in a double Shaker pattern, the right and wrong sides look the same. Be aware, though, that the patterns in this section require more yarn than usual to make.

Brioche-knitted patterns are stretchy. It is recommended that you use smaller needles to get a tighter knit. As a result, these patterns will have a tighter gauge. There are usually more rows in a 4-inch (10-cm) swatch than normal. Keep this in mind when you are combining these stitch patterns with others. Garter stitch patterns or slipped-stitch patterns are good choices to use with brioche patterns.

A very good pattern is the two-color double Shaker pattern on page 37. The "plain" ribbing appears in one color on the front and another color on the back. The look is stunning, but it is not at all complicated to knit. On a circular needle, simply work 2 right side rows and 2 wrong side rows one after the other. All stitches

that have been knitted in the row beforehand without a yarn over are now each slip stitched purlwise with a yarn over. All stitches that have been slip stitched before with a yarn over are now either knitted or purled together with this yarn over.

Double Shaker Knitting: odd number of stitches

Row 1 (wrong side row): Edge stitch, * knit 1 stitch, slip 1 stitch purlwise with 1 yarn over; repeat from *, end with 1 knit stitch, edge stitch.

Row 2 (right side row): Edge stitch, with yarn in back slip 1 stitch purlwise, make 1 yarn over, * knit next stitch together with the yarn over, slip 1 stitch purlwise, make 1 yarn over; repeat from *, edge stitch.

Row 3: Edge stitch, * knit 1 stitch together with the yarn over, with yarn in front slip 1 stitch purlwise, make 1 yarn over; repeat from *, end with knitting together 1 stitch and the yarn over, edge stitch.

Following row 1, repeat rows 2 and 3.

Two-color Double Shaker Knitting: odd number of stitches

This pattern is knitted in rows on a circular needle where 2 right side rows are always followed by 2 wrong side rows. Following the 1st right side row, slide stitches to the right point of the needle and knit the 2nd right side row. Then knit the 3rd row (wrong side), slide the stitches back, and knit the 4th row.

In order to get an equally firm hem, you should purl the edge stitches in all odd-numbered rows and knit them in all even-numbered rows.

Row 1 (right side row), violet: Edge stitch, * purl 1 stitch, slip 1 stitch purlwise with 1 yarn over; repeat from *, end with 1 purl stitch, edge stitch.

Row 2 (right side row), silver: Edge stitch, * slip 1 stitch purlwise with 1 yarn over, knit next stitch together with yarn over; repeat from *, end by slipping 1 stitch purlwise with 1 yarn over, edge stitch.

Row 3 (wrong side row), violet: Edge stitch, knit 1 stitch together with yarn over, * slip 1 stitch purlwise with 1 yarn over, knit 1 stitch together with yarn over; repeat from *, edge stitch.

Row 4 (wrong side row), silver: Edge stitch, slip 1 stitch purlwise with 1 yarn over, * purl 1 stitch together with yarn over, slip 1 stitch purlwise with 1 yarn over; repeat from *, edge stitch.

Row 5 (right side row), violet: Edge stitch, * purl 1 stitch together with yarn over, slip 1 stitch purlwise with 1 yarn over; repeat from *, end by purling together 1 stitch with yarn over, edge stitch.

Following row 1, repeat rows 2–5.

Single Shaker Knitting: odd number of stitches

Row 1 (wrong side row): Edge stitch, * knit 1 stitch, with yarn in front slip 1 stitch purlwise, make 1 yarn over; repeat from *, end with 1 knit stitch, edge stitch.

Row 2: Edge stitch, * purl 1 stitch; knit together the following stitch with the yarn over; repeat from *, end with 1 purl stitch, edge stitch.

Repeat rows 1 and 2.

With this pattern, either the "knit" side (see pattern on the left, which almost looks like the Double Shaker Knitting) or the other side (see pattern below left) can be used for the outside of your work. But the pattern for the "knit" side is meant for the outside.

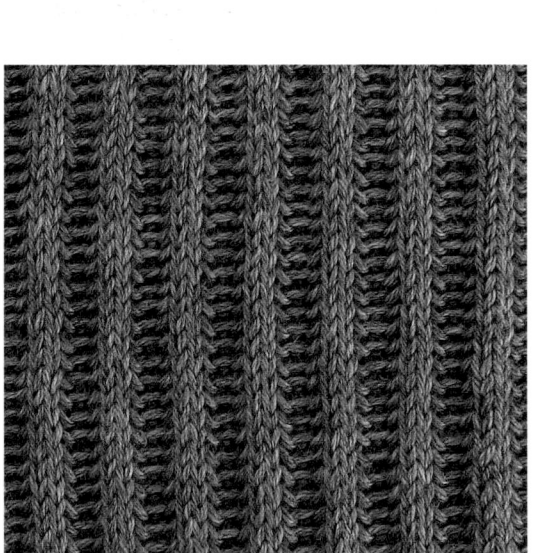

Multiple of 4 sts + 2 + 2 edge sts

Row 1 (wrong side row): Edge stitch, * knit 2 stitches, slip 2 stitches purlwise with 1 yarn over (= work 1 yarn over and slip the following 2 stitches purlwise); repeat from *, end with 2 knit stitches, edge stitch.

Row 2: Edge stitch, slip 2 stitches purlwise with 1 yarn over, * knit together each of the two following stitches with the yarn over (= knit together the 1st stitch with the yarn over, keep the yarn over on the left-hand needle and then knit together the 2nd stitch with the yarn over), slip 2 stitches purlwise with 1 yarn over; repeat from *, edge stitch.

Row 3: Edge stitch, * knit together each of the two following stitches with the yarn over; slip 2 stitches purlwise with 1 yarn over; repeat from *; end by knitting together each of the following 2 stitches with the yarn over, edge stitch.

Following row 1, repeat rows 2 and 3.

Brioche Honeycomb Stitch: even number of stitches

Row 1 (wrong side row): Edge stitch, * slip 1 stitch purlwise with 1 yarn over, knit 1 stitch; repeat from *, edge stitch.

Row 2 (right side row): Edge stitch, * knit 2 stitches, slip the yarn over of the previous row purlwise (yarn behind the yarn over); repeat from *, edge stitch.

Row 3: Edge stitch, * knit together 1 stitch with the yarn over, slip the following stitch purlwise with 1 yarn over; repeat from *, edge stitch.

Row 4: Edge stitch, * knit 1 stitch, slip the yarn over of the previous row purlwise, 1 knit stitch; repeat from *, edge stitch.

Row 5: Edge stitch, * slip 1 stitch purlwise with 1 yarn over, knit the following stitch together with the yarn over; repeat from *, edge stitch.

Following row 1, repeat rows 2–5.

Two-color Brioche Pattern: even number of stitches

Row 1 (wrong side row), silver: Edge stitch, * slip 1 stitch purlwise with 1 yarn over, 1 knit stitch; repeat from *, edge stitch.

Row 2 (right side row), silver: Edge stitch, * knit 2 stitches, slip the yarn over of previous row purlwise (yarn behind the yarn over); repeat from *, edge stitch.

Row 3, violet: Edge stitch, * knit 1 stitch together with the yarn over, slip the following stitch purlwise with 1 yarn over; repeat from *, edge stitch.

Row 4, violet: Edge stitch, * knit 1 stitch, slip the yarn over of the previous row purlwise, knit 1 stitch; repeat from *, edge stitch.

Row 5, silver: Edge stitch, * slip 1 stitch purlwise with 1 yarn over, knit the following stitch together with the yarn over; repeat from *, edge stitch.

Row 6 (right side row), silver: Edge stitch, * knit 2 stitches, slip the yarn over of the previous row purlwise; repeat from *, edge stitch.

Following rows 1 and 2, repeat rows 3–6.

Knitting with 3 colors (see photo on the left) produces a very striking pattern. Here, 2 rows each have been knitted in silver, violet, and rose. Repeat the order of these colors.

Brioche Stitch Patterns

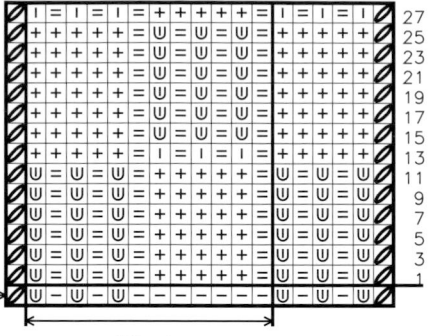

Multiple of 12 sts + 5 + 2 edge sts

The pattern begins with a wrong side row: Repeat the pattern of 12 stitches following the edge stitch and end as drawn. Then work according to the knitting chart for right side rows. On wrong side rows, knit stitches as they are described in the explanation of the knitting symbols. Knit the wrong side row (see arrow) and repeat rows 1–28.

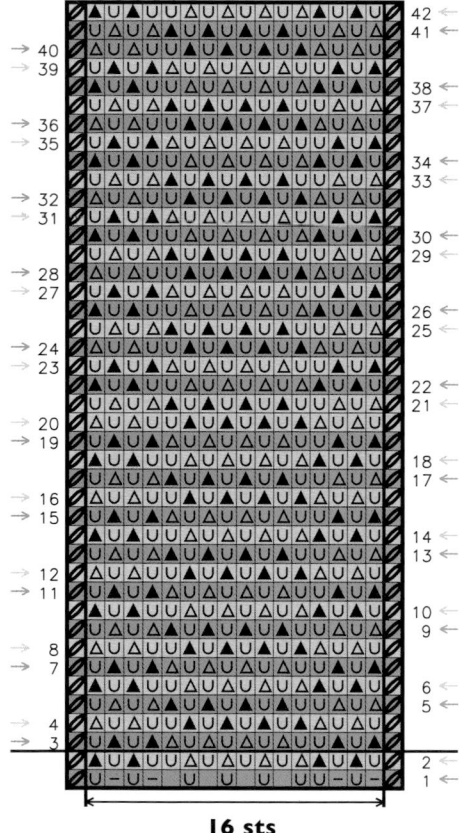

Multiple of 16 sts + 2 edge sts

On right and wrong side rows, work with a circular needle according to the knitting chart and repeat the pattern following the edge stitch. Always knit 2 right side rows and then 2 wrong side rows alternating as indicated in the chart. After the 1st right side row, slip stitches back, leave at right back of work, and knit the 2nd right side row. Then knit the 3rd row (wrong side), slide the stitches back and knit the 4th row, and so on. Following rows 1 and 2, repeat rows 3–42.

Hint: To get firm edge stitches, purl them in odd rows and knit them in even rows.

Panel of 16 sts + 7 + 2 edge sts

The pattern starts with a wrong side row: Following the edge stitch, repeat the pattern of 16 stitches and end as drawn. Then knit on right side rows according to the knitting chart: Begin as indicated in the chart, repeat the pattern and then edge stitch. On wrong side rows, work stitches in pattern or as described in the explanation of the symbols. Knit the wrong side rows (see arrow) and repeat rows 1–8.

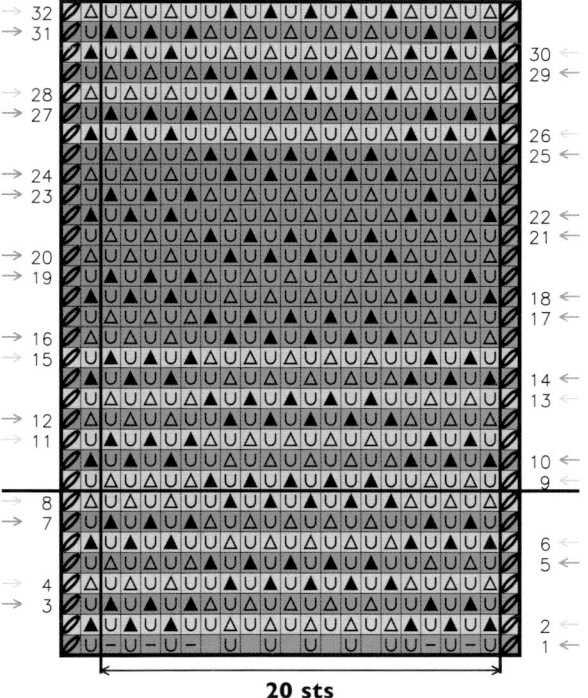

Multiple of 20 sts + 1 + 2 edge sts

On right and wrong side rows, work with a circular needle according to the knitting chart: Begin as indicated in the chart, repeat the pattern and end as drawn. Always knit 2 right side rows and then 2 wrong side rows alternately in the colors indicated in the drawing. Following the 1st right side row, slide stitches to the right point of the needle and knit the 2nd right side row. Then knit the 3rd row (wrong side), slide stitches back and knit the 4th row, and so on. Following rows 1–8, repeat rows 9–32.

Hint: To get firm edge stitches, purl them in odd rows and knit them in even rows.

Brioche Stitch Patterns

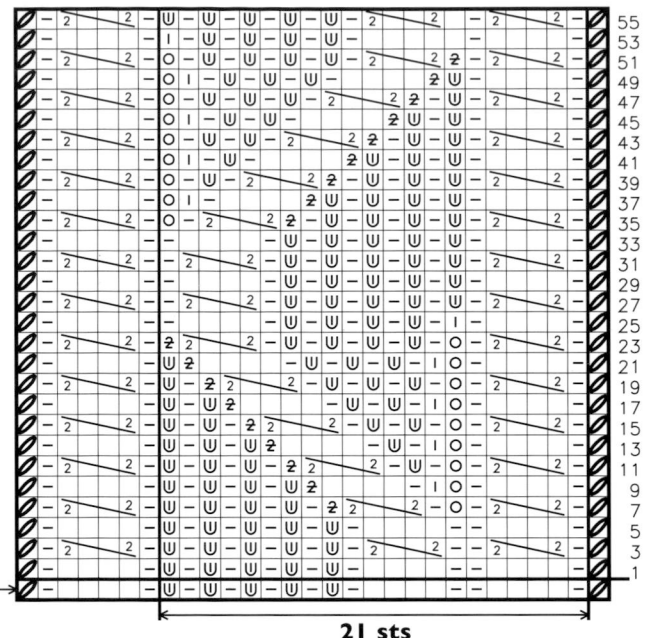

21 sts

Multiple of 21 sts + 6 + 2 edge sts

The pattern starts with a wrong side row, beginning as indicated in the chart. Then repeat the pattern of 21 stitches and edge stitch. After this, knit on right side rows according to the knitting chart. On wrong side rows, work stitches in pattern or as described in the explanation of the symbols. Following the wrong side row (see arrow), repeat rows 1–56.

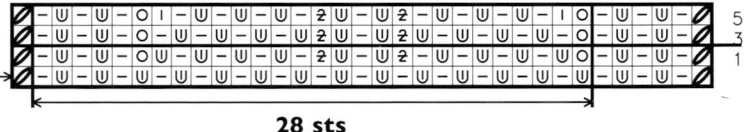

28 sts

Panel of 28 sts + 5 + 2 edge sts

The pattern starts with a wrong side row: Following the edge stitch, repeat the pattern of 28 stitches and end as drawn. Then knit on right side rows according to the knitting chart. Begin as indicated in the chart, repeat the pattern, and end as drawn. On wrong side rows, work stitches in pattern or as described in the explanation of the symbols. Following the wrong side row (see arrow), knit rows 1 and 2 and then repeat rows 3–6.

16 sts

Multiple of 16 sts + 8 + 2 edge sts

The pattern begins with a wrong side row: Begin as indicated in the chart and repeat the pattern of 16 stitches and edge stitch. Then knit on right side rows according to the knitting chart. On wrong side rows, knit stitches as described in the explanation of the symbols. Following the wrong side row (see arrow), repeat rows 1–24.

= Hold 4 stitches on a cable needle in front of the work, slip 1 stitch purlwise with 1 yarn over, knit 1 stitch together with the yarn over, slip 1 stitch purlwise with 1 yarn over, knit 1 stitch together with the yarn over, then slip 1 stitch purlwise with 1 yarn over off the cable needle, knit 1 stitch together with the yarn over, slip 1 stitch purlwise with 1 yarn over, knit 1 stitch together with the yarn over.

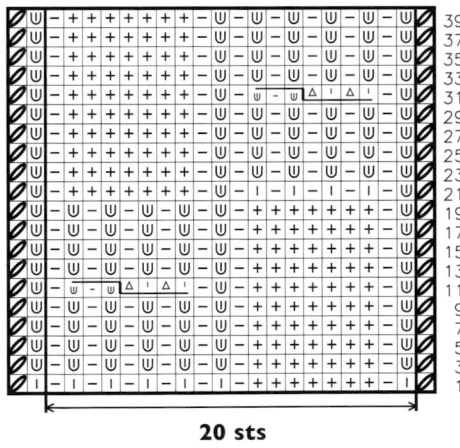

20 sts

Multiple of 20 sts + 1 + 2 edge sts

On right side rows, work according to knitting chart. Beginning as indicated in the chart, repeat the pattern and end as drawn. On wrong side rows, work stitches in pattern or as described in the explanation of the symbols. Repeat rows 1–40.

= Hold 3 stitches on a cable needle in front of the work, knit 1 stitch, purl 1 stitch together with the yarn over, knit 1 stitch, purl 1 stitch together with the yarn over, then knit 1 stitch together with the yarn over from the cable needle, 1 purl stitch, knit 1 stitch together with the yarn over.

Brioche Stitch Patterns

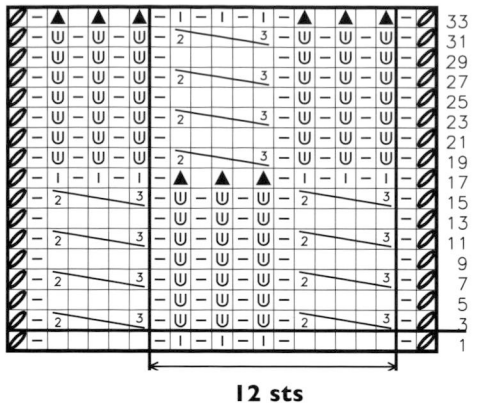

12 sts

Multiple of 12 sts + 7 + 2 edge sts

On right side rows, work according to the knitting chart. Beginning as indicated in the chart, repeat the pattern and end as drawn. On wrong side rows, work stitches in pattern or as described in the explanation of the symbols.
Following rows 1 and 2, repeat rows 3–34.

= Hold 2 stitches on a cable needle in front of the work, 3 knit stitches, then knit the stitches from the cable needle.

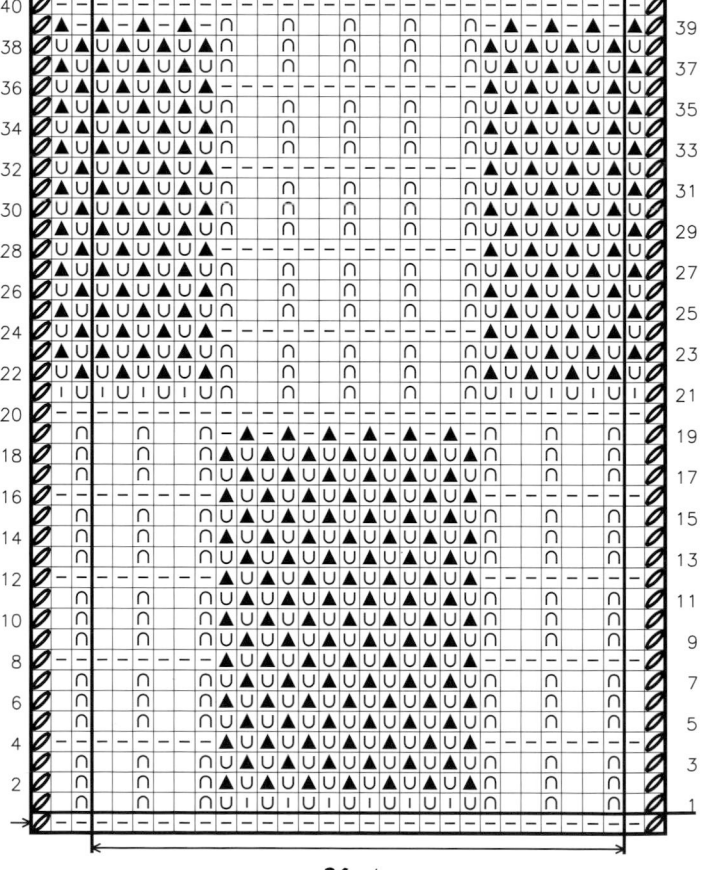

26 sts

Multiple of 26 sts + 3 + 2 edge sts

The pattern starts with a wrong side row. Beginning as indicated in the chart, repeat the pattern of 26 stitches and end as drawn. Then knit right and wrong side rows according to the knitting chart. Following the wrong side row (see arrow), repeat rows 1–40.

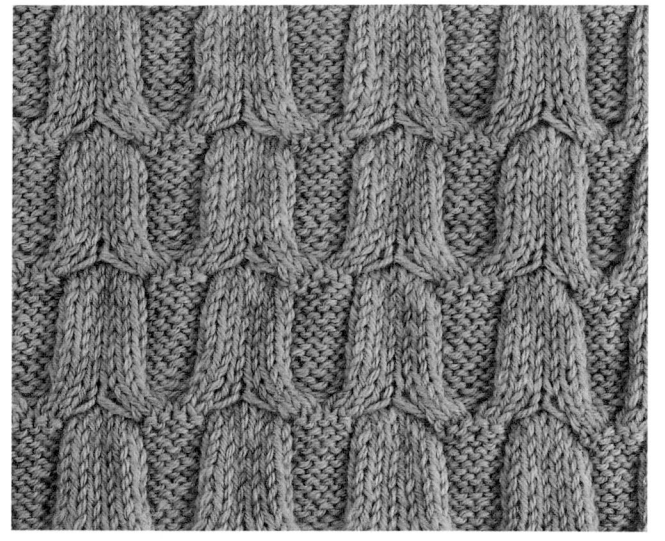

Cable Patterns

Cable patterns are timeless and beautiful in their endless variations. They are commonly used on fisherman sweaters, but they can also be used in all sorts of fabulous combinations with yarn ranging from fine cotton to chunky wool.

Cables are produced by crossing stitches to the right or left. You will get twisted "cords" from two strands, braid cables from three or more strands, in addition to multifold bands, diagonal strips, diamonds, chains, or zigzag lines.

The stitches are crossed with the help of a cable needle. One or several stitches are lifted from the left-hand needle onto the cable needle and are held, depending on the pattern, to the front or back of the work. A groove in the cable needle prevents the stitches from sliding off. Then, in correspondence to the pattern, the stitches of the left-hand needle are first knitted and then the stitches from the cable needle.

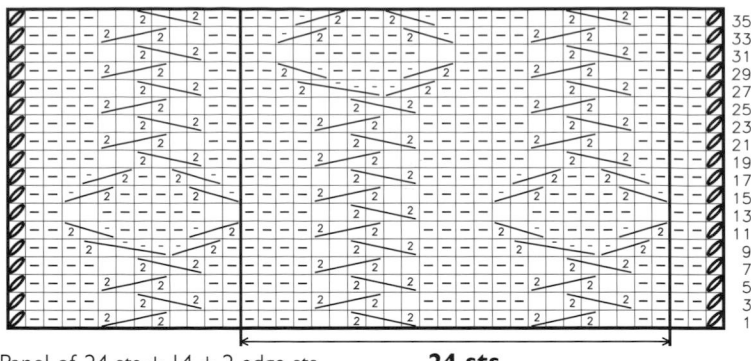

Panel of 24 sts + 14 + 2 edge sts **24 sts**

On right side rows, work according to the knitting chart. Beginning as indicated in the chart, repeat the pattern of 24 stitches and end as drawn. On wrong side rows, work stitches in pattern. Repeat rows 1–36.

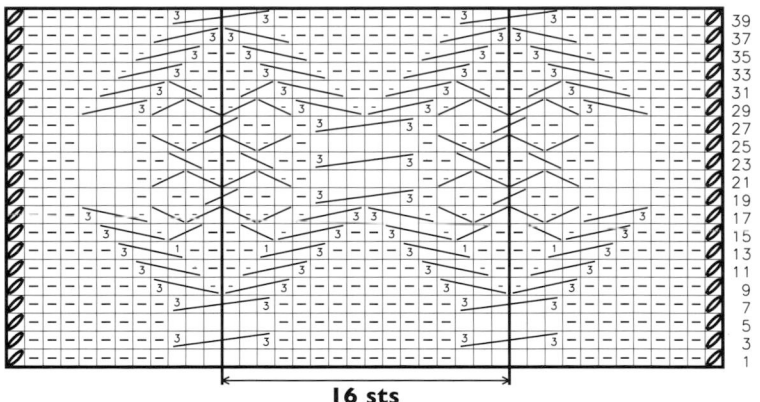

Multiple of 16 sts + 6 + 2 edge sts **16 sts**

On right side rows, work according to the knitting chart. Beginning as indicated in the chart, repeat the pattern of 16 stitches and end as drawn. On wrong side rows, work stitches in pattern. Repeat rows 1–40.

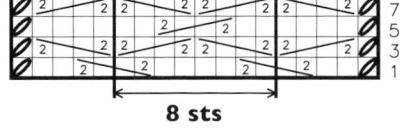

8 sts

Multiple of 8 sts + 2 edge sts

On right side rows, work according to the knitting chart. Beginning as indicated in the chart, repeat the pattern of 8 stitches and end as drawn. On wrong side rows, work stitches in pattern. Repeat rows 1–8.

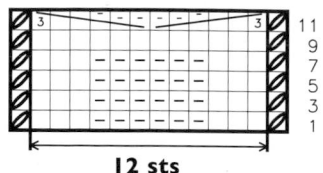

Multiple of 12 sts + 2 edge sts

On right side rows, work according to the knitting chart. Following the edge stitch, repeat the pattern of 12 stitches and then edge stitch. On wrong side rows, work stitches in pattern. Repeat rows 1–12.

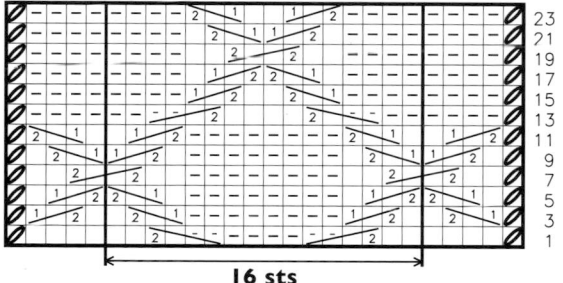

Multiple of 16 sts + 8 + 2 edge sts

On right side rows, work according to the knitting chart. Beginning as indicated in the chart, repeat the pattern of 16 stitches and end as drawn. On wrong side rows, purl all stitches. Repeat rows 1–24.

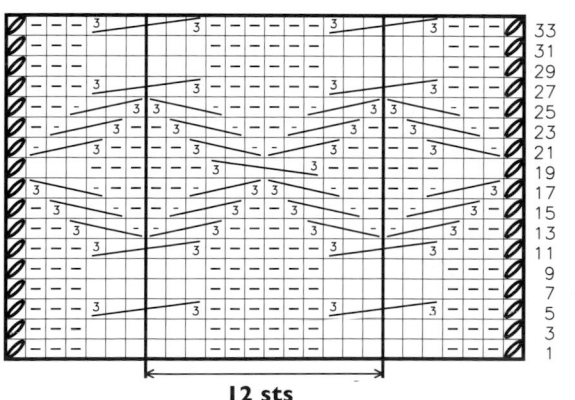

Multiple of 12 sts + 2 edge sts

On right side rows, work according to the knitting chart. Beginning as indicated in the chart, repeat the pattern of 12 stitches and end as drawn. On wrong side rows, work stitches in pattern. Repeat rows 1–34.

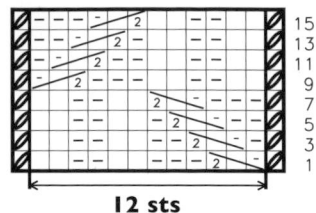

12 sts

Multiple of 12 sts + 2 edge sts

On right side rows, work according to the knitting chart. Following the edge stitch, repeat the pattern of 12 stitches and then edge stitch. On wrong side rows, work stitches in pattern. Repeat rows 1–16.

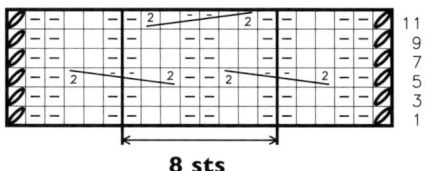

8 sts

Multiple of 8 sts + 2 + 2 edge sts

On right side rows, work according to the knitting chart. Beginning as indicated in the chart, repeat the pattern of 8 stitches and end as drawn. On wrong side rows, work stitches in pattern. Repeat rows 1–12.

4 sts

Multiple of 4 sts + 2 edge sts

On right side rows, work according to the knitting chart. Beginning as indicated in the chart, repeat the pattern of 4 stitches and end as drawn. On wrong side rows, work stitches in pattern. Repeat rows 1–4.

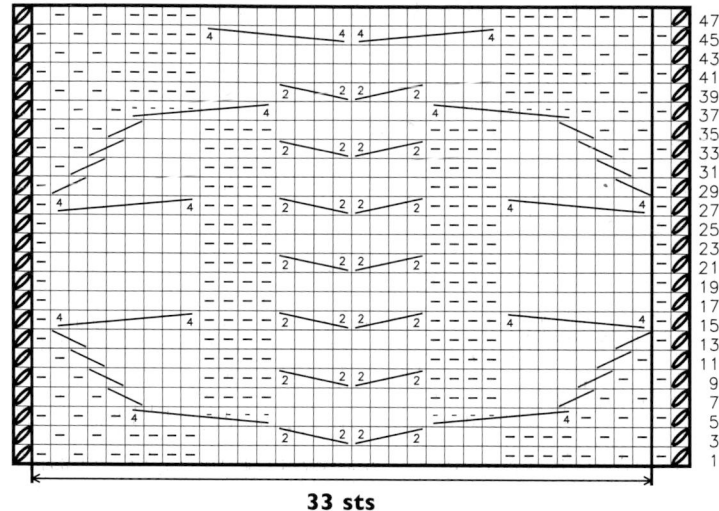

33 sts

Multiple of 33 sts + 1 + 2 edge sts

On right side rows, work according to the knitting chart. Beginning as indicated in the chart, repeat the pattern of 33 stitches and then edge stitch. On wrong side rows, work stitches in pattern. Repeat rows 1–48.

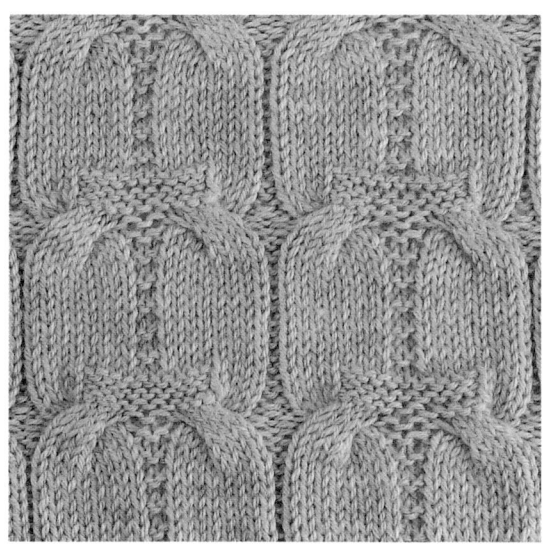

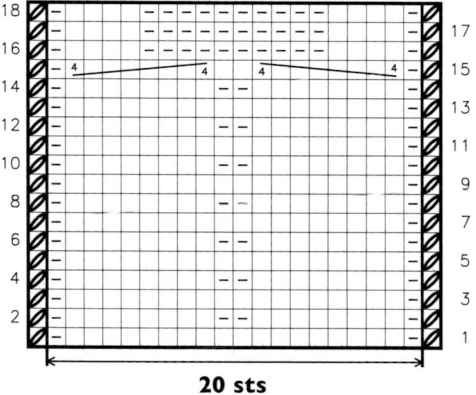

20 sts

Multiple of 20 sts + 2 edge sts

On right and wrong side rows, work according to the knitting chart. Following the edge stitch, repeat the pattern of 20 stitches and then edge stitch. Repeat rows 1–18.

Cable Patterns

Cable strands for 46 stitches

On right side rows, knit the cable strand for 46 stitches according to the knitting chart. On wrong side rows, work stitches in pattern. Following rows 1 and 2, repeat rows 3–26.

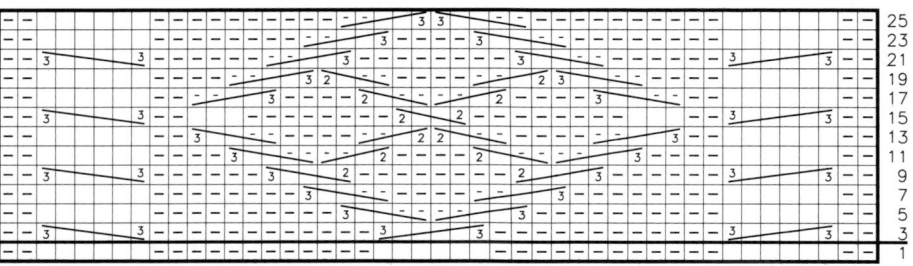

Cable strands for 56 stitches

On right side rows, work according to the knitting chart. On wrong side rows, work stitches in pattern. Repeat rows 1–24.

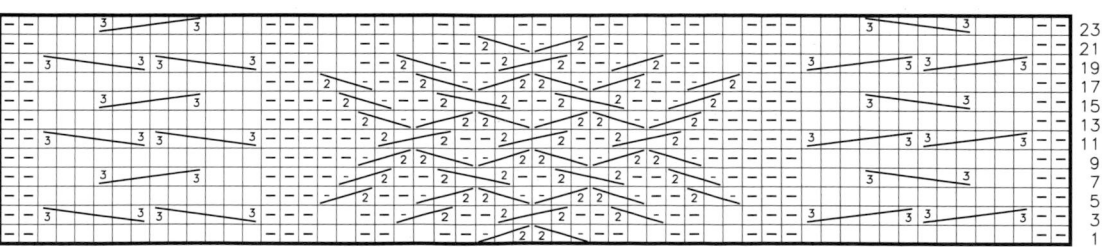

Cable strands for 47 stitches

On right side rows, work according to the knitting chart. On wrong side rows, work stitches in pattern. Following rows 1 and 2, repeat rows 3–22.

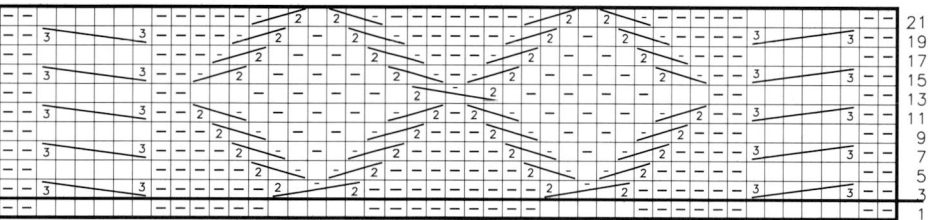

Cable strands for 47 stitches

On right side rows, work according to the knitting chart. On wrong side rows, work stitches in pattern. Following rows 1 and 2, repeat rows 3–34.

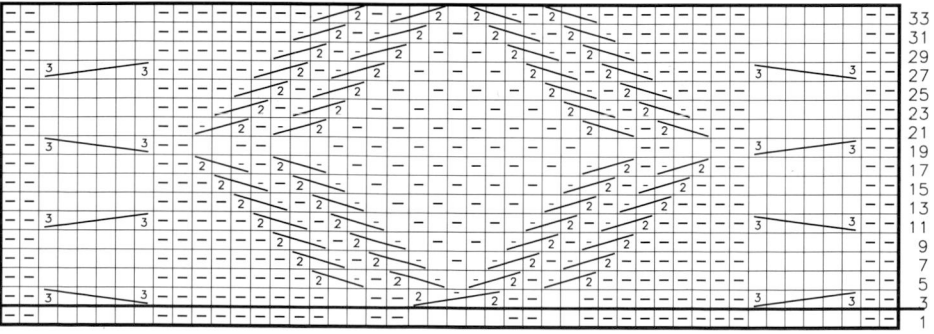

Lace Patterns

Hand-knitted sweaters can look elegant with these "see through" patterns. Lace patterns, which are also called filigree patterns, are made from an elaborate combination of yarn overs and stitches worked together. The result can be geometrical shapes, such as diamonds or zigzags, as well as nature motifs, such as a leaf or a flower.

The lace patterns can be worked as individual motifs or along vertical or horizontal panels to give a touch of elegance to each sweater. For this reason, softer, more delicate yarns should be used when making these patterns. These yarns could be mercerized cotton, viscose, or even silk. Lace patterns can also have a distinctive look if they are knitted from mohair yarn even though the pattern will not stand out as prominently as with the other yarns.

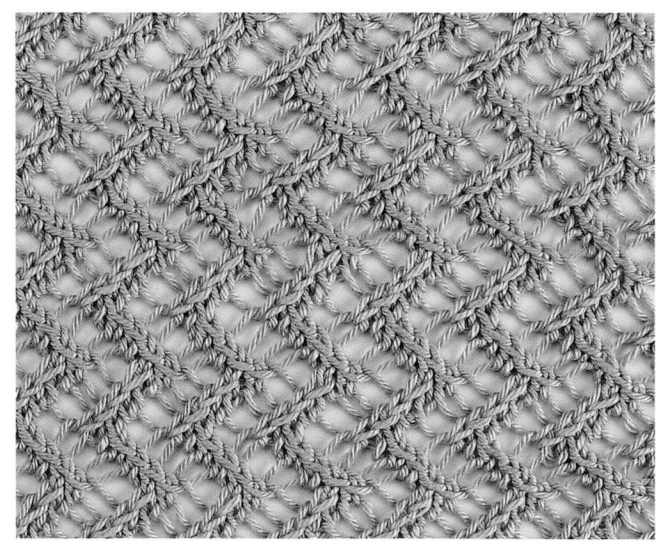

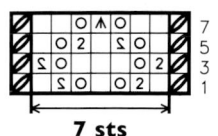

7 sts

Multiple of 7 sts + 2 edge sts

On right side rows, work according to the knitting chart. Following the edge stitch, repeat the pattern of 7 stitches and then edge stitch. On wrong side rows, purl all stitches and yarn overs. Repeat rows 1–8.

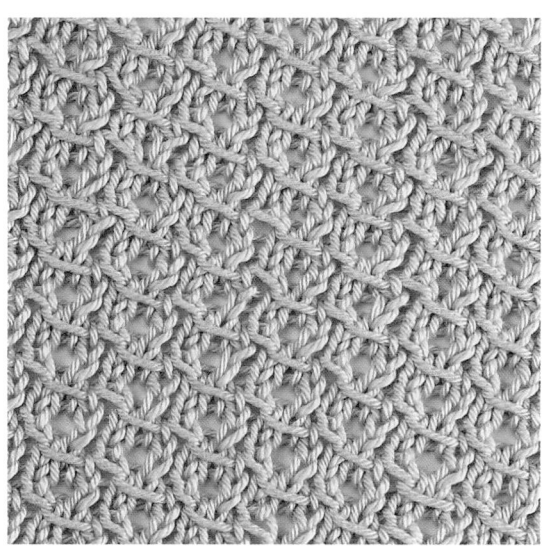

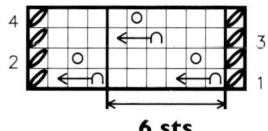

6 sts

Multiple of 6 sts + 3 + 2 edge sts

On right and wrong side rows, work according to the knitting chart. On right side rows, repeat the pattern of 6 stitches after the edge stitch and end as drawn. Repeat rows 1–4.

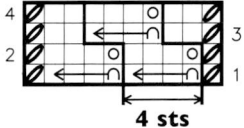

4 sts

Multiple of 4 sts + 2 edge sts

On right and wrong side rows, work according to the knitting chart. Beginning as indicated in the chart, repeat the pattern of 4 stitches and end as drawn. Repeat rows 1–4.

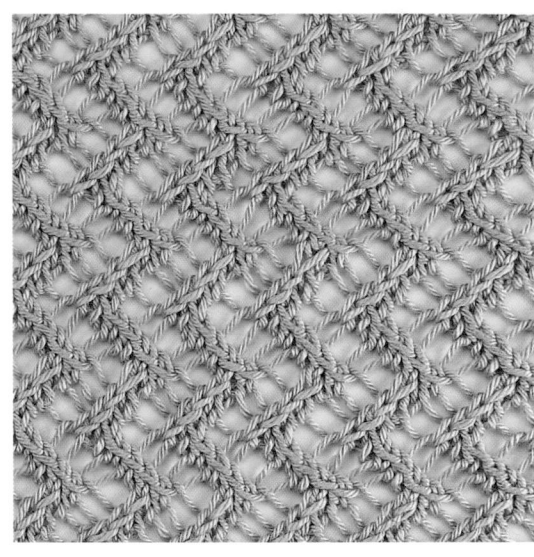

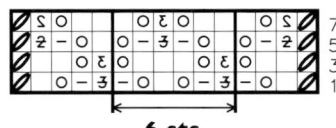

4 sts

Multiple of 4 sts + 3 + 2 edge sts

On right and wrong side rows, work according to the knitting chart. Beginning as indicated in the chart, repeat the pattern of 4 stitches and end as drawn. Repeat rows 1–8.

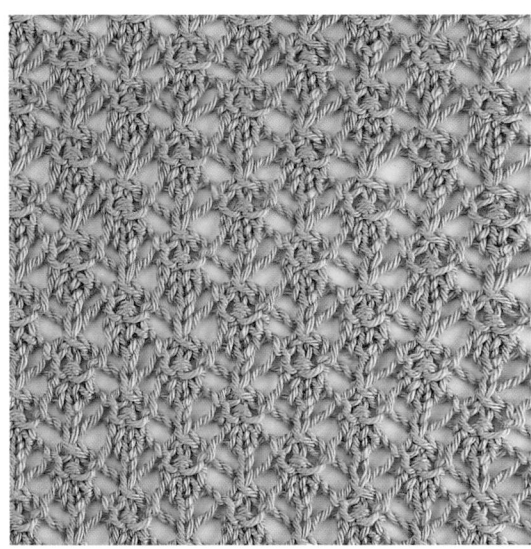

6 sts

Multiple of 6 sts + 1 + 2 edge sts

On right side rows, work according to the knitting chart. Beginning as indicated in the chart, repeat the pattern of 6 stitches and end as drawn. On wrong side rows, work stitches in pattern and purl yarn overs. Repeat rows 1–8.

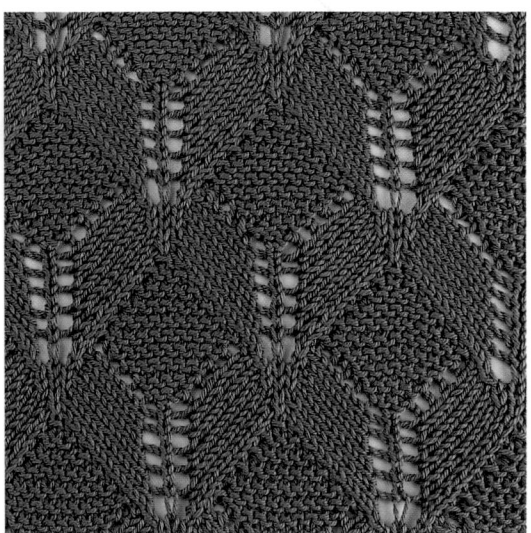

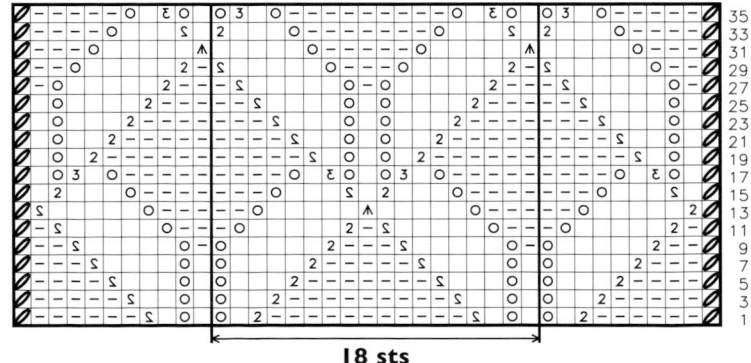

18 sts

Multiple of 18 sts + 1 + 2 edge sts

On right side rows, work according to the knitting chart. Beginning as indicated in the chart, repeat the pattern of 18 stitches and end as drawn. On wrong side rows, purl all stitches and yarn overs. Repeat rows 1–36.

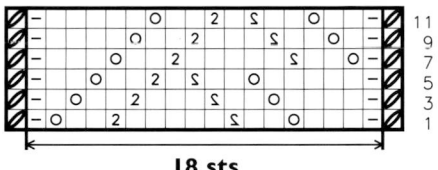

14 sts

Multiple of 14 sts + 1 + 2 edge sts

On right side rows, work according to the knitting chart. Beginning as indicated in the chart, repeat the pattern of 14 stitches and end as drawn. On wrong side rows, work stitches in pattern and purl yarn overs. Repeat rows 1–26.

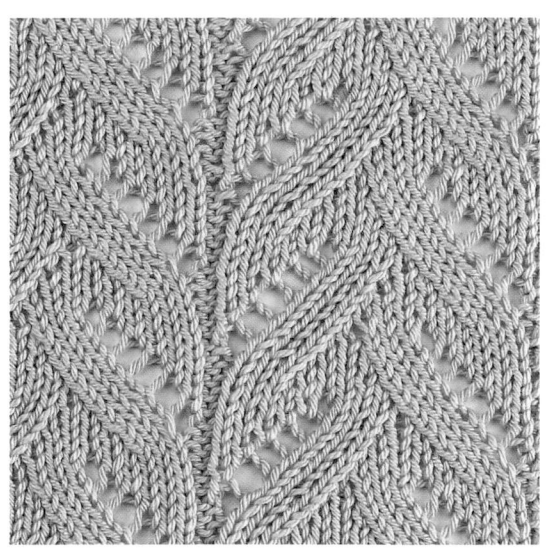

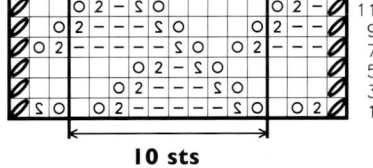

18 sts

Multiple of 18 sts + 2 edge sts

On right side rows, work according to the knitting chart. Following the edge stitch, repeat the pattern of 18 stitches and then edge stitch. On wrong side rows, purl all stitches and yarn overs. Repeat rows 1–12.

10 sts

Multiple of 10 sts + 5 + 2 edge sts

On right side rows, work according to the knitting chart. Beginning as indicated in the chart, repeat the pattern of 10 stitches and end as drawn. On wrong side rows, work stitches in pattern and purl yarn overs. Repeat rows 1–12.

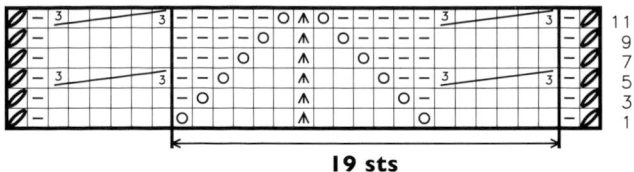

19 sts

Multiple of 19 sts + 8 + 2 edge sts

On right side rows, work according to the knitting chart. Beginning as indicated in the chart, repeat the pattern of 19 stitches and end as drawn. On wrong side rows, work stitches in pattern and purl yarn overs. Repeat rows 1–12.

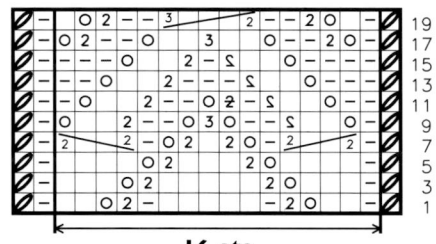

16 sts

Multiple of 16 sts + 1 + 2 edge sts

On right side rows, work according to the knitting chart. Following the edge stitch, repeat the pattern of 16 stitches and end as drawn. On wrong side rows, work stitches in pattern and purl yarn overs. Repeat rows 1–20.

= Hold 3 stitches on a cable needle in the back of the work, knit 2 stitches, then knit stitches from the cable needle.

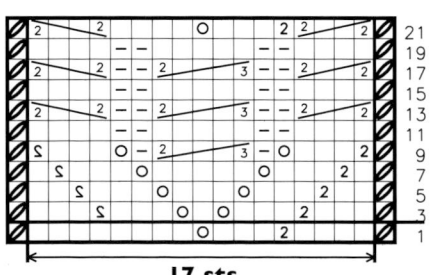

17 sts

Multiple of 17 sts + 2 edge sts

On right side rows, work according to the knitting chart. Following the edge stitch, repeat the pattern of 17 stitches and then edge stitch. On wrong side rows, work stitches in pattern and purl yarn overs. Following rows 1 and 2, repeat rows 3–22.

= Hold 2 stitches on a cable needle in the back of the work, knit 3 stitches, then knit stitches from the cable needle.

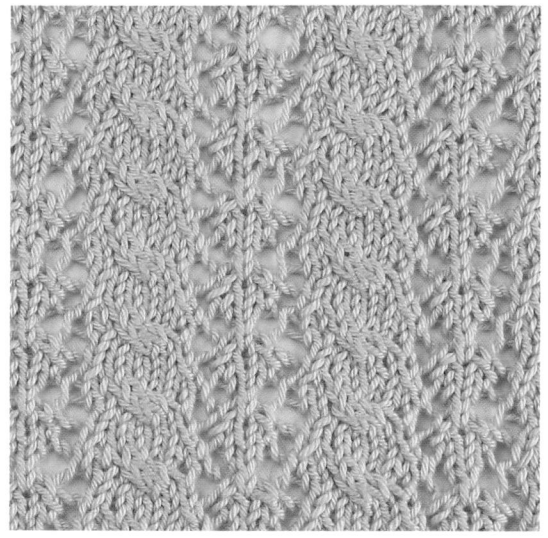

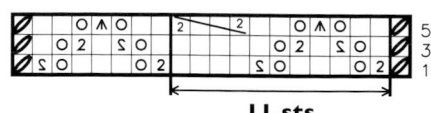

Multiple of 11 sts + 7 + 2 edge sts

On right side rows, work according to the knitting chart. Following the edge stitch, repeat the pattern of 11 stitches and end as drawn. On wrong side rows, purl all stitches and yarn overs. Repeat rows 1–6.

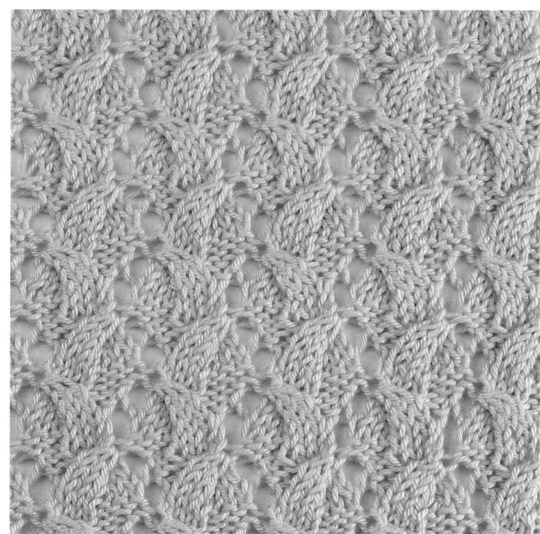

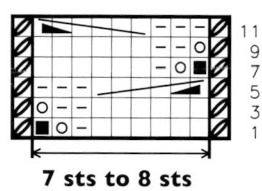

7 sts to 8 sts to 9 sts

Attention: The number of stitches alternates!

Cast on multiple of 7 sts + 2 edge sts

On right side rows, work according to the knitting chart. Following the edge stitch, repeat the pattern and then edge stitch.

On wrong side rows, work stitches in pattern and purl yarn overs. Repeat rows 1–12.

 = Hold 3 stitches on a cable needle in front of the work, knit 3 stitches, then work the 3 stitches of the cable needle together by knitting into the back of stitches.

 = Hold 3 stitches on a cable needle in the back of the work, knit 3 stitches together, then knit the stitches from the cable needle.

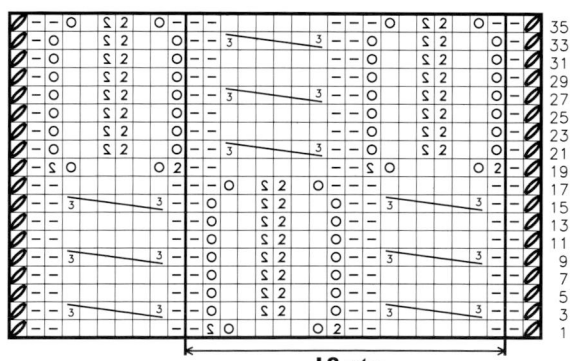

Multiple of 18 sts + 10 + 2 edge sts

On right side rows, work according to the knitting chart. Beginning as indicated in the chart, repeat the pattern of 18 stitches and end as drawn. On wrong side rows, work stitches in pattern and purl yarn overs. Repeat rows 1–36.

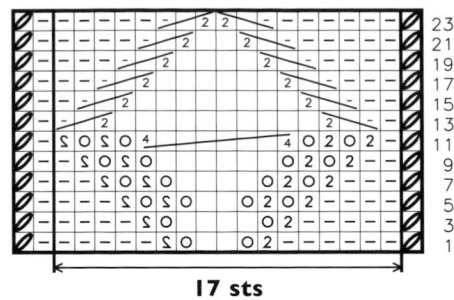

17 sts

Multiple of 17 sts + 1 + 2 edge sts

On right side rows, work according to the knitting chart. Following the edge stitch, repeat the pattern of 17 stitches and end as drawn. On wrong side rows, work stitches in pattern and purl yarn overs. Repeat rows 1–24.

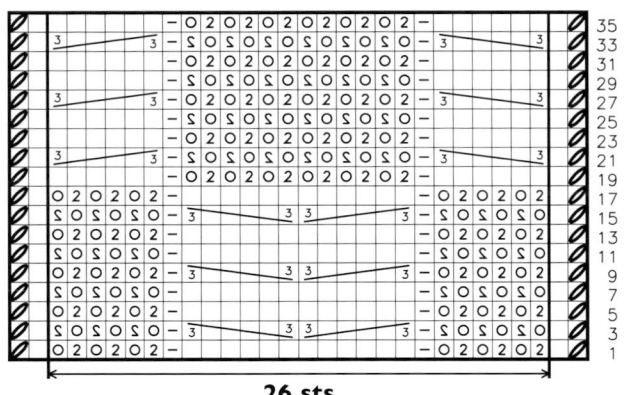

26 sts

Multiple of 26 sts + 2 + 2 edge sts

On right side rows, work according to the knitting chart. Beginning as indicated in the chart, repeat the pattern of 26 stitches and end as drawn. On wrong side rows, work stitches in pattern and purl yarn overs. Repeat rows 1–36.

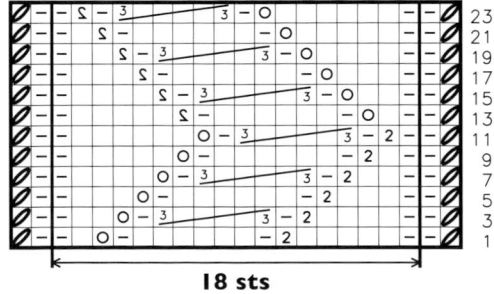

18 sts

Multiple of 18 sts + 2 + 2 edge sts

On right side rows, work according to the knitting chart. Beginning as indicated in the chart, repeat the pattern of 18 stitches and end as drawn. On wrong side rows, work stitches in pattern and purl yarn overs. Repeat rows 1–24.

Multiple of 20 sts + 1 + 2 edge sts

On right side rows, work according to the knitting chart. Beginning as indicated in the chart, repeat the pattern of 20 stitches and end as drawn. On wrong side rows, work stitches in pattern and purl yarn overs. Repeat rows 1–36.

 = Hold 2 stitches on a cable needle in the back of the work, knit 3 stitches, then knit the stitches from the cable needle.

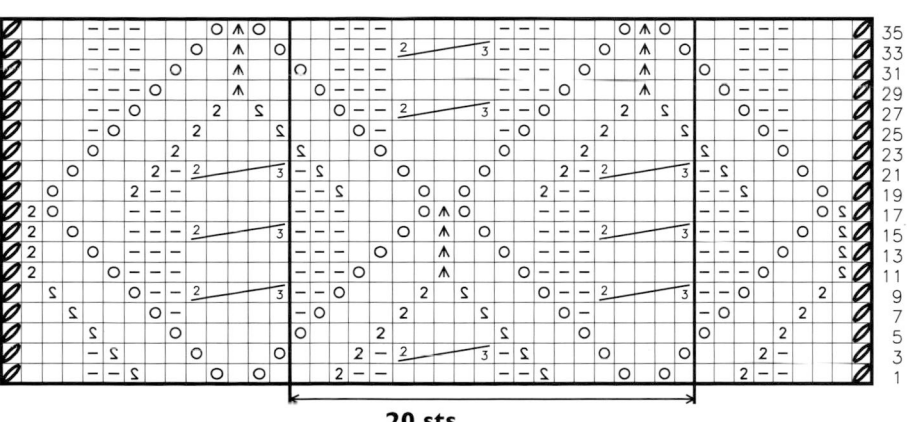

20 sts

12 sts

Multiple of 12 sts + 1 + 2 edge sts

On right side rows, work according to the knitting chart. Beginning as indicated in the chart, repeat the pattern of 12 stitches and end as drawn. On wrong side rows, work stitches in pattern and purl yarn overs. Repeat rows 1–20.

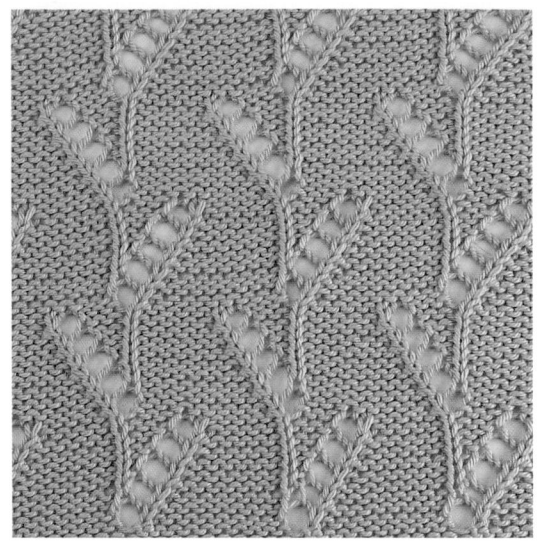

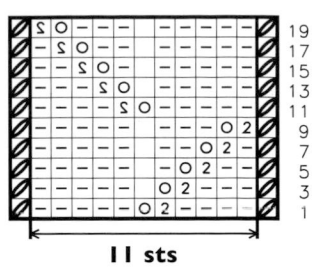

11 sts

Multiple of 11 sts + 2 edge sts

On right side rows, work according to the knitting chart. Following the edge stitch, repeat the pattern of 11 stitches and then edge stitch. On wrong side rows, work stitches in pattern and purl yarn overs. Repeat rows 1–20.

20 sts

Multiple of 20 sts + 1 + 2 edge sts

On right side rows, work according to the knitting chart. Beginning as indicated in the chart, repeat the pattern of 20 stitches and end as drawn. On wrong side rows, work stitches in pattern and purl yarn overs. Repeat rows 1–28.

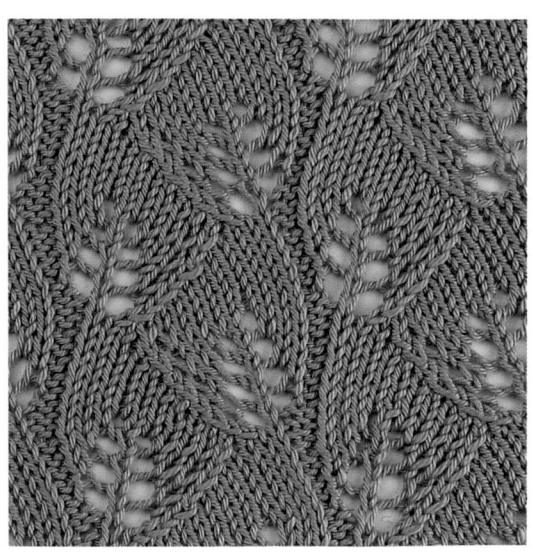

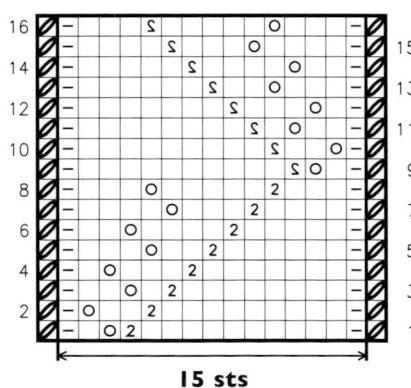

15 sts

Multiple of 15 sts + 2 edge sts

On right and wrong side rows, work according to the knitting chart. Following the edge stitch, repeat the pattern of 15 stitches and then edge stitch. On wrong side rows, work stitches in pattern and purl yarn overs. Repeat rows 1–16.

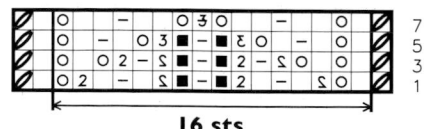

Attention: The number of stitches alternates!

Multiple of 16 sts + 1 + 2 edge sts

On right side rows, work according to the knitting chart. Following the edge stitch, repeat the pattern and end as drawn. On wrong side rows, work stitches in pattern and purl yarn overs. Repeat rows 1–8.

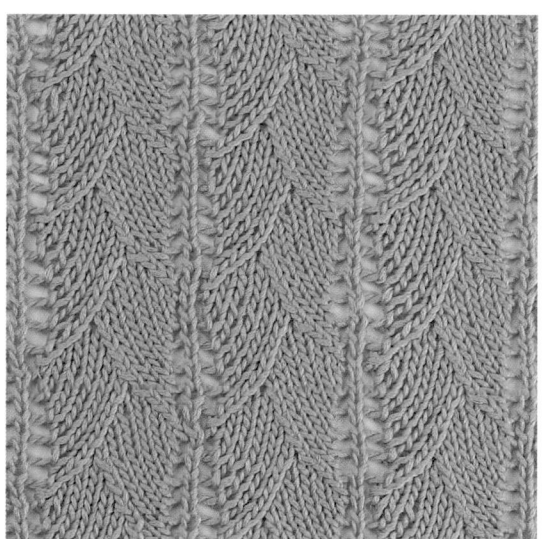

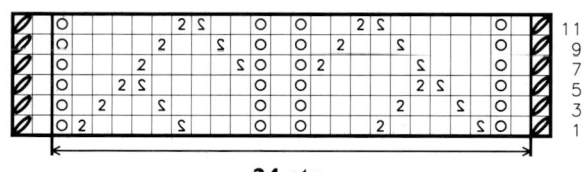

Multiple of 24 sts + 1 + 2 edge sts

On right side rows, work according to the knitting chart. Following the edge stitch, repeat the pattern of 24 stitches and end as drawn. On wrong side rows, work stitches in pattern and purl yarn overs. Repeat rows 1–12.

Multiple of 8 sts + 1 + 2 edge sts

On right side rows, work according to the knitting chart. Beginning as indicated in the chart, repeat the pattern of 8 stitches and end as drawn. On wrong side rows, work stitches in pattern and purl yarn overs. Repeat rows 1–12.

Lace Patterns

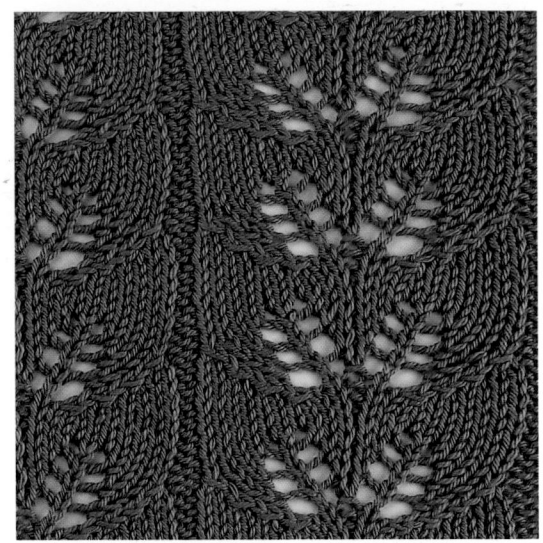

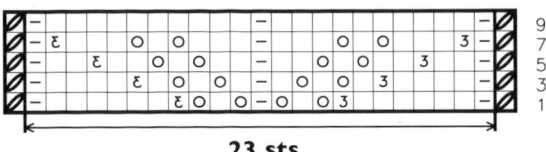

23 sts

Multiple of 23 sts + 2 edge sts

On right side rows, work according to the knitting chart. Following the edge stitch, repeat the pattern of 23 stitches and then edge stitch. On wrong side rows, work stitches in pattern and purl yarn overs. Repeat rows 1–10.

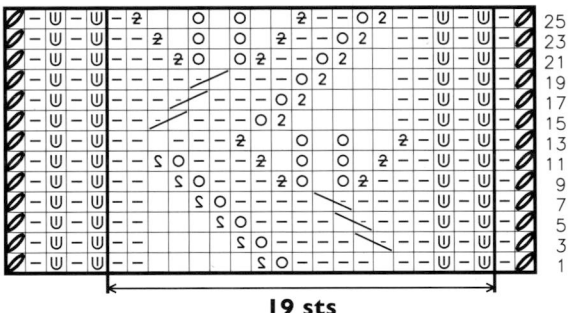

19 sts

Multiple of 19 sts + 5 + 2 edge sts

On right side rows, work according to the knitting chart. Beginning as indicated in the chart, repeat the pattern of 19 stitches and end as drawn. On wrong side rows, work stitches in pattern, or as described in the explanation of symbols, and purl yarn overs. Repeat rows 1–26.

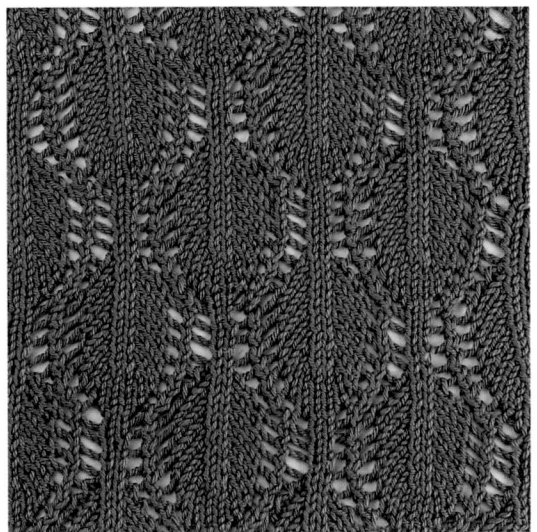

16 sts

Multiple of 16 sts + 2 edge sts

On right side rows, work according to the knitting chart. Following the edge stitch, repeat the pattern of 16 stitches and then edge stitch. On wrong side rows, purl all stitches and yarn overs. Repeat rows 1–28.

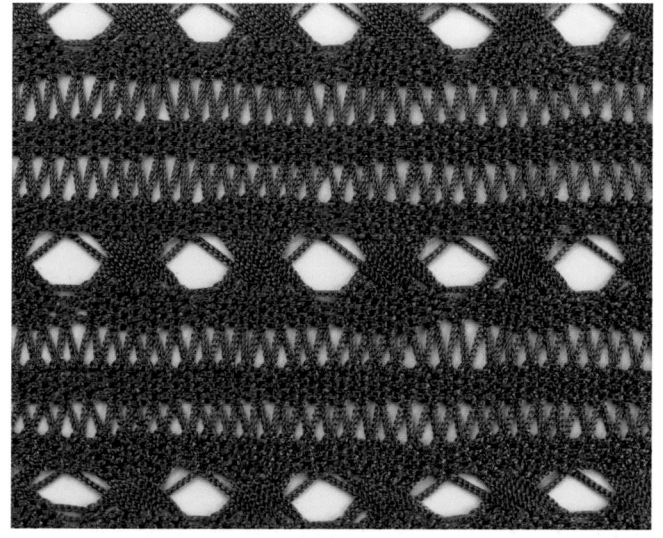

Openwork Patterns

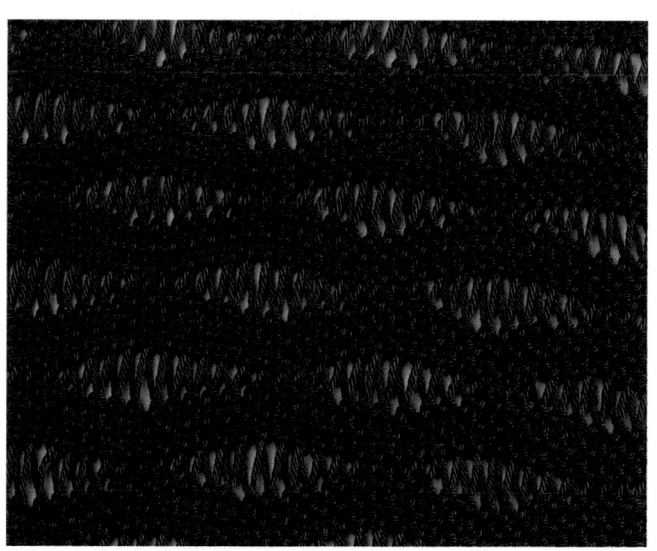

With these patterns, you will certainly make a "cool" fashion statement. The effect, however, does not come from just yarn overs and working stitches together. In some patterns, you will use larger needles and stretched stitches. A few intermediary rows knitted with a smaller size needle will keep the shape of work. The results are very stylish sweaters and tops made from ribbon or microfiber yarns in no time at all.

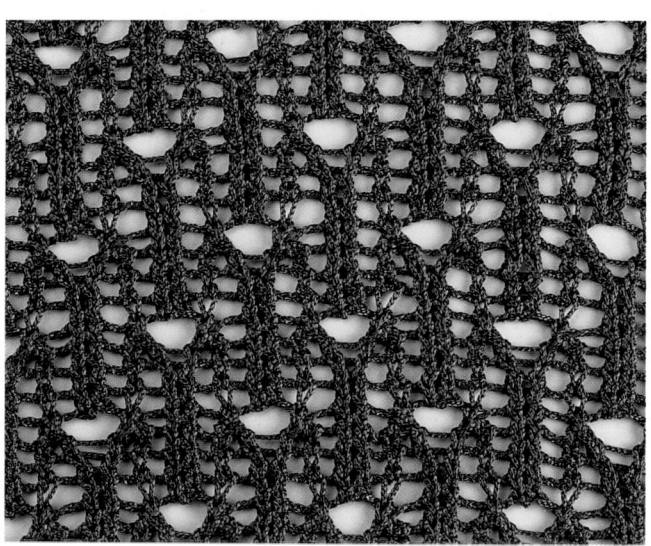

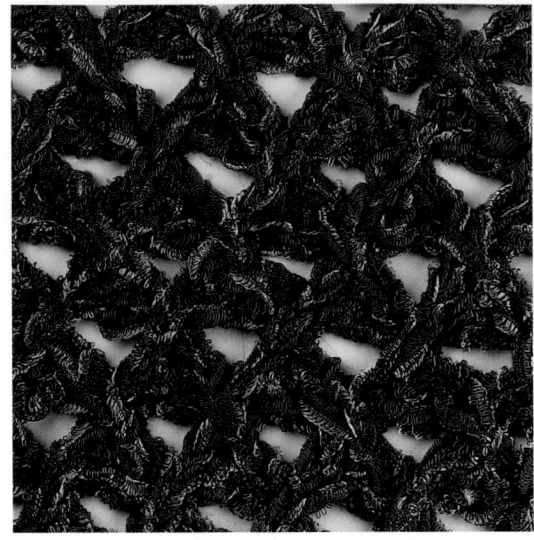

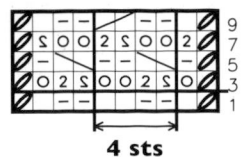

4 sts

Multiple of 4 sts + 2 edge sts

On right side rows, knit stitches according to the knitting chart. Beginning as indicated in the chart, repeat the pattern of 4 stitches and end as drawn. On wrong side rows, work stitches in pattern; from the 2 yarn overs, purl 1 stitch, knit 1 stitch, and then purl the single yarn over. Following rows 1 and 2, repeat rows 3–10.

This pattern is worked with a ribbon yarn, knitting needles in sizes 3, and 10–11, and a thin crochet yarn for size 10.

Multiple of 6 sts + 2 edge sts

Row 1 (right side row), ribbon yarn, needles 10–11: Purl all stitches.

Row 2, ribbon yarn, needles 10–11: Edge stitch, * purl 1 yarn over and 1 stitch; repeat from *, edge stitch.

Row 3, ribbon yarn, needles 10–11: Knit all stitches, drop the yarn overs, and stretch the stitch.

Row 4, crochet yarn, needle 3: Edge stitch, * purl 5 stitches together, then work 5 stitches in the following stitch (alternately 1 purl stitch and then 1 yarn over); repeat from *, edge stitch.

Row 5, crochet yarn, needle 3: Purl all stitches.

Row 6 and 7, ribbon yarn, needles 10–11: Repeat rows 2 and 3.

Row 8, crochet yarn, needle 3: Edge stitch, * work 5 stitches in the following stitch, then purl 5 stitches together; repeat from *, edge stitch.

Row 9, crochet yarn, needle 3: Purl all stitches.

Row 10, ribbon yarn, needles 10–11: Repeat row 2.

Following rows 1 and 2, repeat rows 3–10.

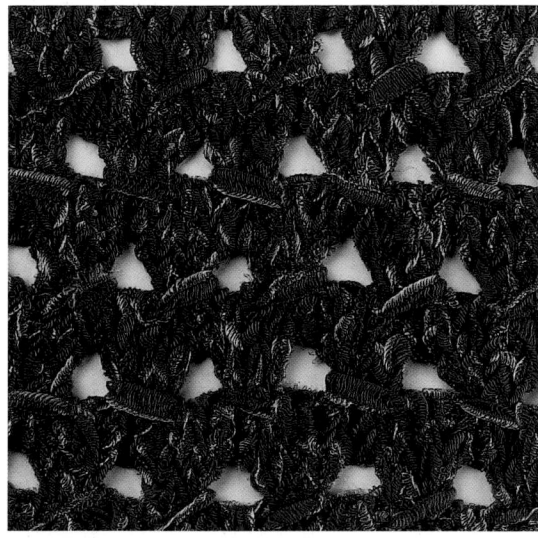

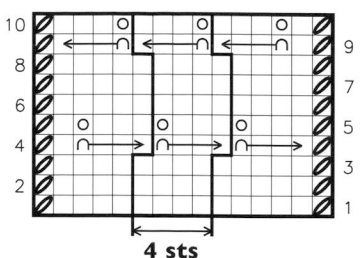

4 sts

Multiple of 4 sts + 1 + 2 edge sts

On right and wrong side rows, work according to the knitting chart. Beginning as indicated in the chart, repeat the pattern of 4 stitches and end as drawn. On the following wrong side row, purl the yarn overs. On the following right side row, knit the yarn overs. Repeat rows 1–10.

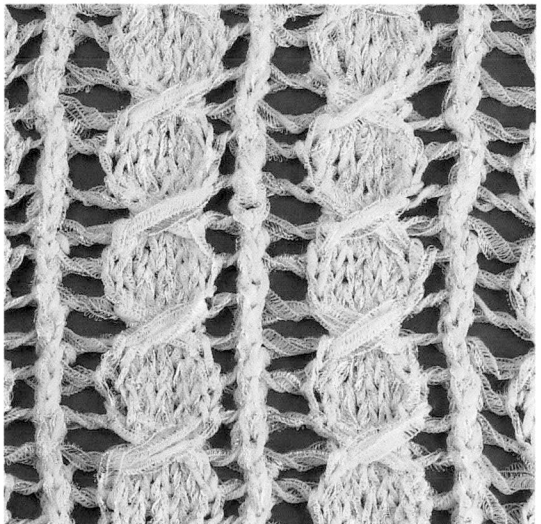

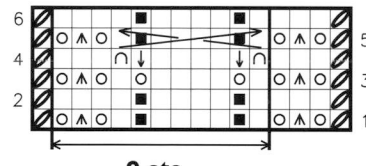

9 sts

Multiple of 9 sts + 3 + 2 edge sts

On right and wrong side rows, work according to the knitting chart. On right side rows, begin as indicated in the chart, repeat the pattern of 9 stitches and then edge stitch. Repeat rows 1–6.

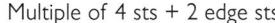 = Hold 5 stitches on a cable needle in the back of the work, knit 1 stitch, then place 1st stitch of the cable needle onto the 2nd cable needle in front of the 1st cable needle; knit the 4 stitches of the 1st cable needle and then knit the stitch of the 2nd cable needle.

Multiple of 4 sts + 2 edge sts

Row 1 (wrong side row): Edge stitch, * purl 2 stitches together, make 1 yarn over, purl 2 stitches; repeat from *, edge stitch.

Row 2: Edge stitch, * work a single decrease by passing 1 stitch over the other (slip 1 stitch knitwise, knit 1 stitch, and pass the slipped stitch over the knitted stitch), make 1 yarn over, knit the following yarn over and next stitch; repeat from *, edge stitch.

Row 3: Edge stitch, * purl 2 stitches together, make 1 yarn over, purl the following yarn over and next stitch; repeat from *, edge stitch.

Following row 1, repeat rows 2 and 3.

Openwork Patterns

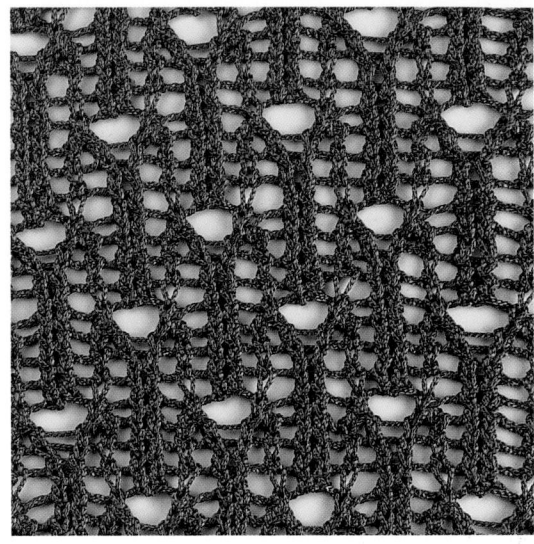

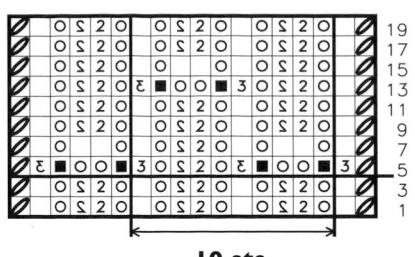

10 sts

Multiple of 10 sts + 6 + 2 edge sts

On right side rows, work according to the knitting chart. Beginning as indicated in the chart, repeat the pattern of 10 stitches and end as drawn. On wrong side rows, purl all stitches and yarn overs; from the 2 yarn overs, purl 1 stitch and knit the other. Following rows 1–4, repeat rows 5–20.

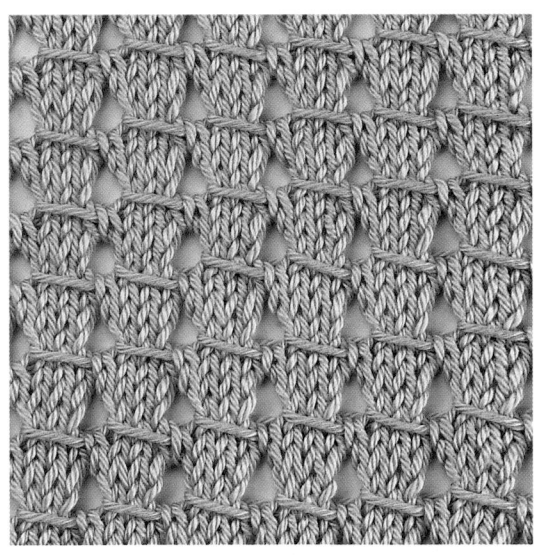

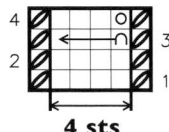

4 sts

Multiple of 4 sts + 2 edge sts

On right and wrong side rows, work according to the knitting chart. Following the edge stitch, repeat the pattern of 4 stitches and then edge stitch. Knit yarn overs in the following right side row. Repeat rows 1–4.

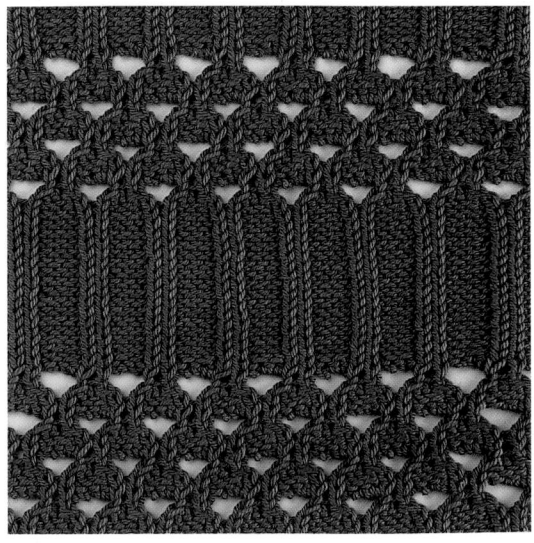

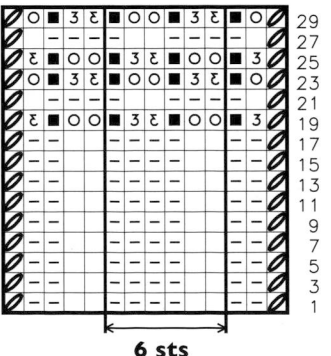

6 sts

Multiple of 6 sts + 2 edge sts

On right side rows, work according to the knitting chart. Beginning as indicated in the chart, repeat the pattern of 6 stitches and end as drawn. On wrong side rows, work stitches in pattern; from the 2 yarn overs, knit 4 stitches (alternately 1 purl stitch, then 1 knit stitch). Repeat rows 1–30.

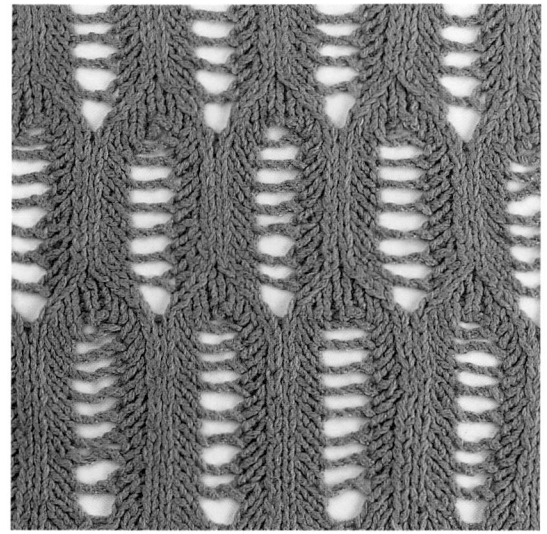

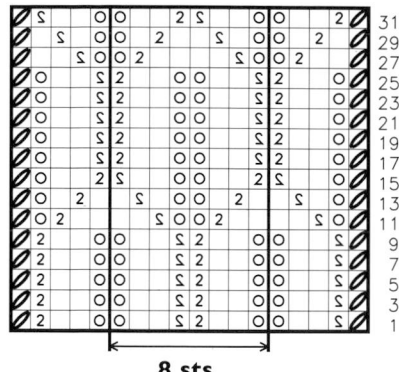

8 sts

Multiple of 8 sts + 2 edge sts

On right side rows, work according to the knitting chart. Beginning as indicated in the chart, repeat the pattern of 8 stitches and end as drawn. On wrong side rows, purl all stitches; from the 2 yarn overs, purl 1 stitch and then knit 1 stitch. Repeat rows 1–32.

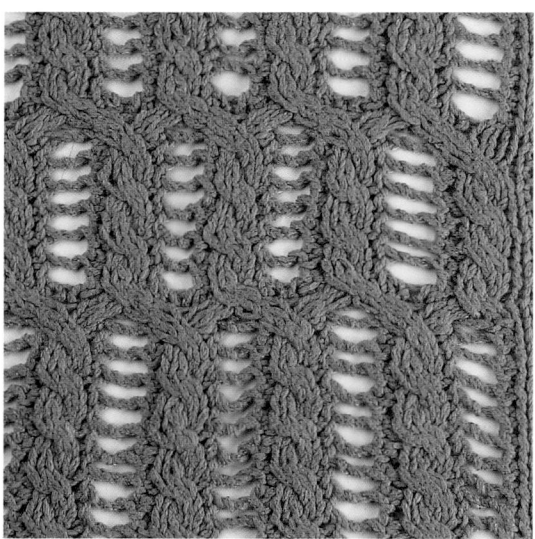

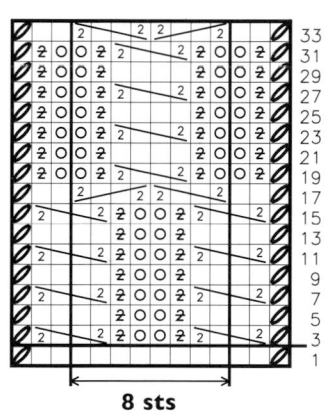

8 sts

Multiple of 8 sts + 4 + 2 edge sts

On right side rows, work according to the knitting chart. Beginning as indicated in the chart, repeat the pattern of 8 stitches and end as drawn. On wrong side rows, work stitches in pattern; from the 2 yarn overs, purl 1 stitch and then knit 1 stitch. Following rows 1 and 2, repeat rows 3–34.

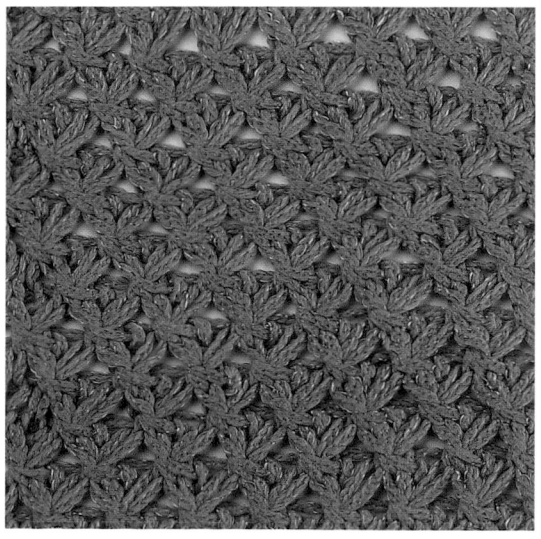

Multiple of 3 sts + 1 + 2 edge sts

Row 1 (right side row): Edge stitch, * make 1 knot: knit into the back of 3 stitches together twisted, but leave the stitches on the needle; make 1 yarn over and once again knit 3 stitches together twisted; then slip stitches off the needle; repeat from *, end with 1 knit stitch, edge stitch.
Row 2: Purl all stitches.
Row 3: Edge stitch, knit 1 stitch, * make 1 knot; repeat from *, edge stitch.
Row 4: Purl all stitches.
Row 5: Edge stitch, knit 2 stitches, * make 1 knot; repeat from *; end with 2 knit stitches, edge stitch.
Row 6: Purl all stitches.

Repeat rows 1–6.

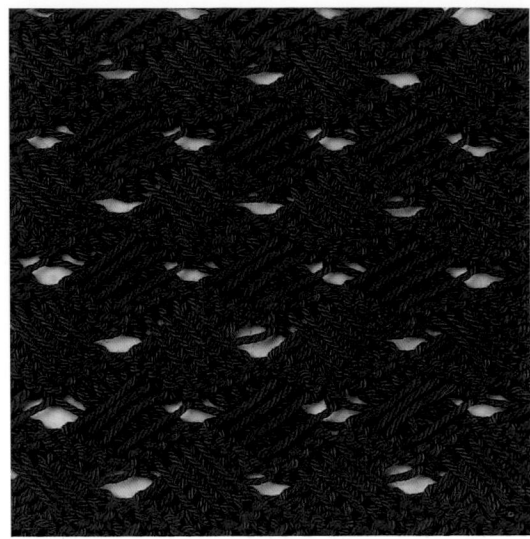

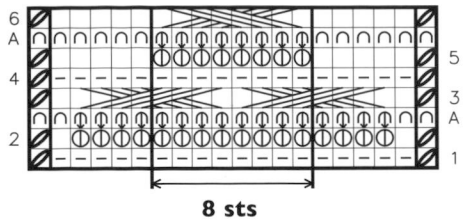

Multiple of 8 sts + 2 + 2 edge sts

The pattern is worked in rows with a circular needle. On right and wrong side rows, work according to the knitting chart. Beginning as indicated in the chart, repeat the pattern of 8 stitches and end as drawn. In the rows marked with the letter "A," all stitches are only slipped purlwise and the yarn overs dropped. Afterwards, slip the stitches back to the other end of the needle and continue knitting. Repeat rows 1–6.

= On right side rows: From the left-hand needle, pass stitches 5 to 8 over the first 4 stitches and hold in front. Then knit each stitch—at first, stitches 5 to 8 and then stitches 1 to 4.

= On wrong side rows: From the left-hand needle, pass stitches 5 to 8 over the first 4 stitches and hold in front. Then purl each stitch—at first, stitches 5 to 8 and then stitches 1 to 4.

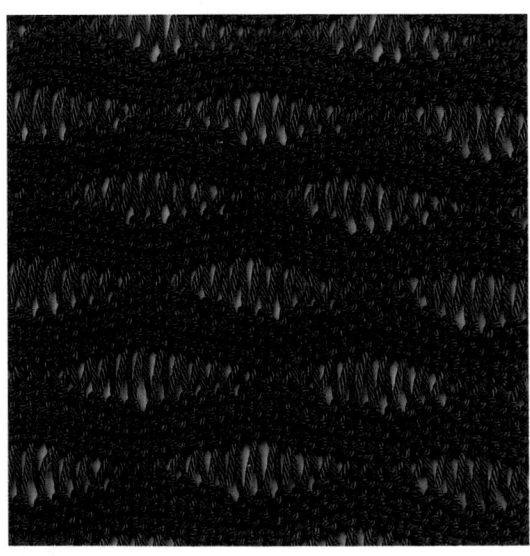

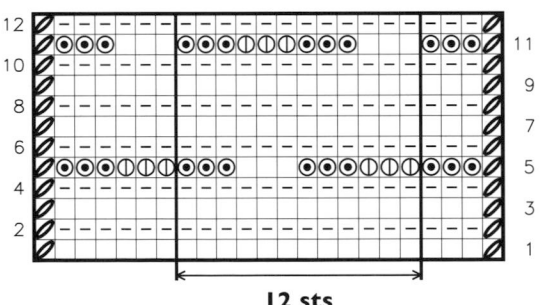

Multiple of 12 sts + 9 + 2 edge sts

On right and wrong side rows, work according to the knitting chart. Beginning as indicated in the chart, repeat the pattern of 12 stitches and end as drawn. In rows 6 and 12, knit all stitches and drop yarn overs. Repeat rows 1–12.

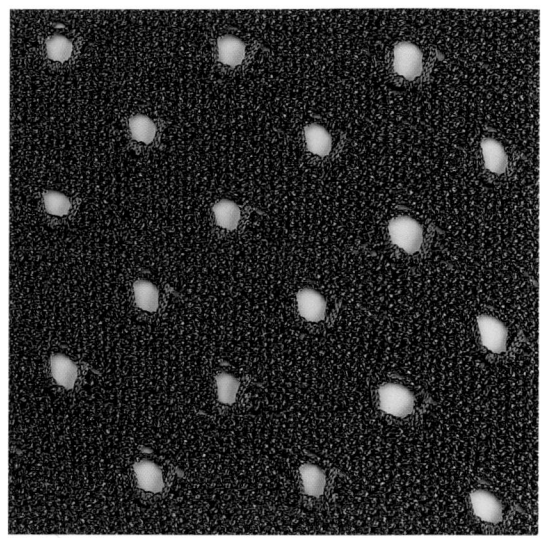

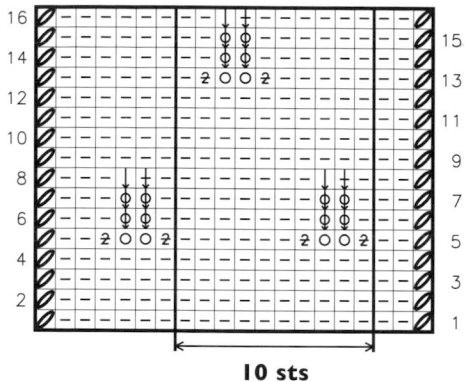

Multiple of 10 sts + 8 + 2 edge sts

On right and wrong side rows, work according to the knitting chart. Beginning as indicated in the chart, repeat the pattern of 10 stitches and end as drawn. Repeat rows 1–16.

⏚ = Drop the yarn over of the previous row and work 1 new yarn over for it.

⎍⎍ = Drop the 2 last yarn overs off the needle. You will now have 3 running threads. Take the threads onto the left-hand needle; purl 1 stitch and then knit 1 stitch from them. Pass the right-hand needle under all running threads.

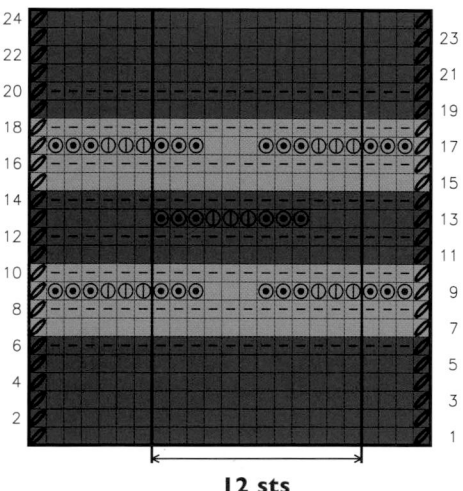

Multiple of 12 sts + 9 + 2 edge sts

On right and wrong side rows, work according to the knitting chart. Beginning as indicated in the chart, repeat the pattern of 12 stitches and end as drawn. Knit all stitches in rows 10, 14, and 18 and drop yarn overs. Repeat rows 1–24.

Openwork Patterns

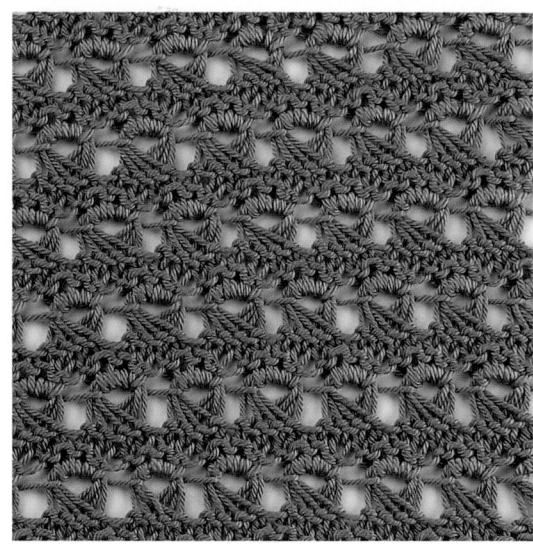

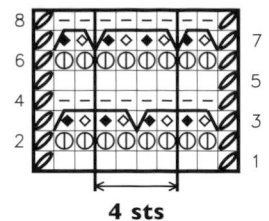

4 sts

Multiple of 4 sts + 2 edge sts

On right and wrong side rows, work according to the knitting chart. Beginning as indicated in the chart, repeat the pattern of 4 stitches and end as drawn. In each 2nd and 6th row, between the edge stitches, knit each stitch with 2 yarn overs. Repeat rows 1–8.

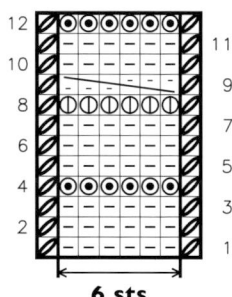

6 sts

Multiple of 6 sts + 2 edge sts

On right and wrong side rows, work according to the knitting chart. Following the edge stitch, repeat the pattern of 6 stitches and end as drawn. After rows 4 and 12, purl all stitches and drop yarn overs. In each 9th row, work stitches as described below. Repeat rows 1–12.

= Slip the following 6 stitches purlwise and drop yarn overs. Afterwards, lift stitches back onto the left-hand needle and cross them: Hold 3 stitches on a cable needle in front of the work, purl 3 stitches and then purl the stitches from the cable needle.

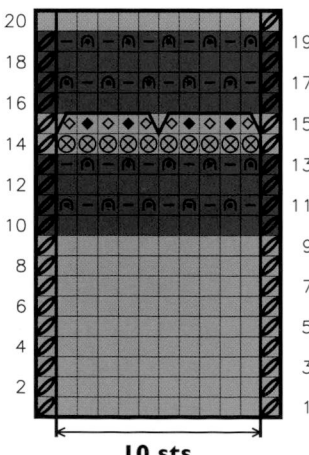

10 sts

Multiple of 10 sts + 2 edge sts

On right and wrong side rows, work according to the knitting chart. Following the edge stitch, repeat the pattern of 10 stitches and then edge stitch. Repeat rows 1–20.

Jacquard Patterns

Jacquard, or Norwegian, patterns have a long tradition. These multicolored geometrical patterns, which are famous in Norwegian sweaters and those from the British Isles, are valued as more than decorative elements: they are particularly thick and warm because at least one of the yarns stretches across the wrong side of the work and, thus, strengthens the knitting. The diamonds on the yokes of Norwegian sweaters, hats, and gloves are famous. But flower and animal motifs or simple decorative borders can also be knitted in the Jacquard style. Many of these classic patterns were probably originated by weavers. The term "Jacquard pattern" hints at this connection because similar patterns have been worked since the beginning of the 19th century on a Jacquard machine, an automatic draw loom developed by Joseph Marie Jacquard.

Jacquard patterns are worked in stockinette stitch with two or more different-color yarns at the same time. The yarn that is not being used is loosely carried along behind the stitches being worked. It is important that these "floats" are handled with regular tension in order to keep the shape and stretch of the knitted work. If you are working with thinner yarn, the "float" should not stretch more than four to five stitches; with thicker yarn, the "float" should not stretch more than three to four stitches. If there is a greater distance between the stitches of one color, then you should occasionally cross the two working yarns in the back in order to avoid having large hanging yarns. The edge stitches are worked with both yarns so that even the last stitches of the color that is not knitted to the edge come out clean and even.

30 sts

Multiple of 30 sts + 1 + 2 edge sts

On right and wrong side rows, work in stockinette stitch in Jacquard technique according to the knitting pattern. Repeat the pattern of 30 stitches following the edge stitch and end as drawn with edge stitch. Repeat rows 1–30.

16 sts

Multiple of 16 sts + 1 + 2 edge sts

On right and wrong side rows, work in stockinette stitch in Jacquard technique according to the knitting pattern. Following the edge stitch, repeat the pattern and end as drawn with edge stitch. Following rows 1–35, repeat rows 36–41.

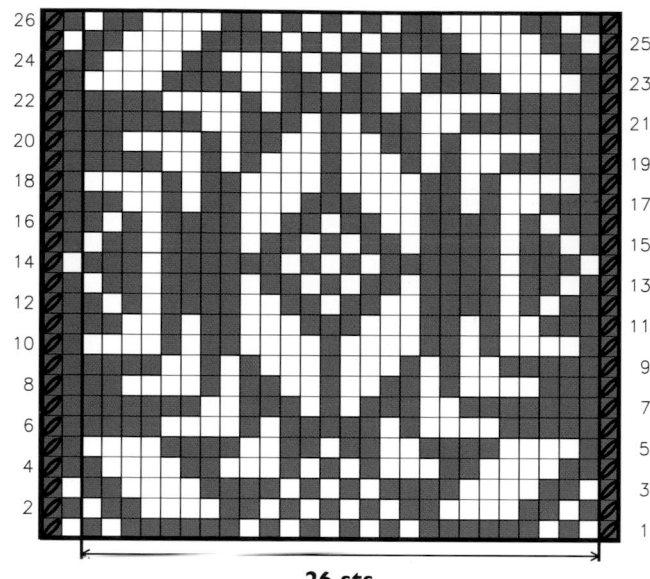

26 sts

Multiple of 26 sts + 1 + 2 edge sts

On right and wrong side rows, work in stockinette stitch in Jacquard technique according to the knitting pattern. On right side rows, repeat the pattern of 26 stitches following the edge stitch and end as drawn with edge stitch. Repeat rows 1–26.

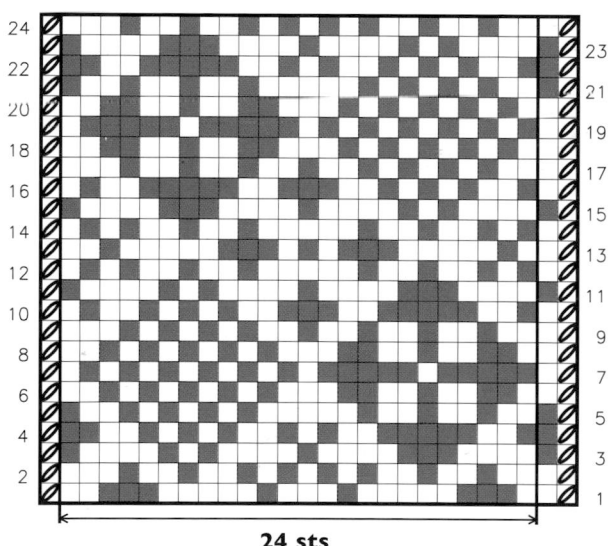

24 sts

Multiple of 24 sts + 1 + 2 edge sts

On right and wrong side rows, work in stockinette stitch in Jacquard technique according to the knitting pattern. On right side rows, following the edge stitch, begin as indicated in the chart, repeat the pattern of 24 stitches and then edge stitch. Repeat rows 1–24.

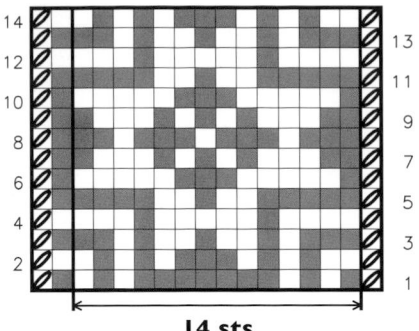

14 sts

Multiple of 14 sts + 1 + 2 edge sts

On right and wrong side rows, work in stockinette stitch in Jacquard technique according to the knitting pattern. On right side rows, following the edge stitch, repeat the pattern of 14 stitches and end as drawn. Repeat rows 1–14.

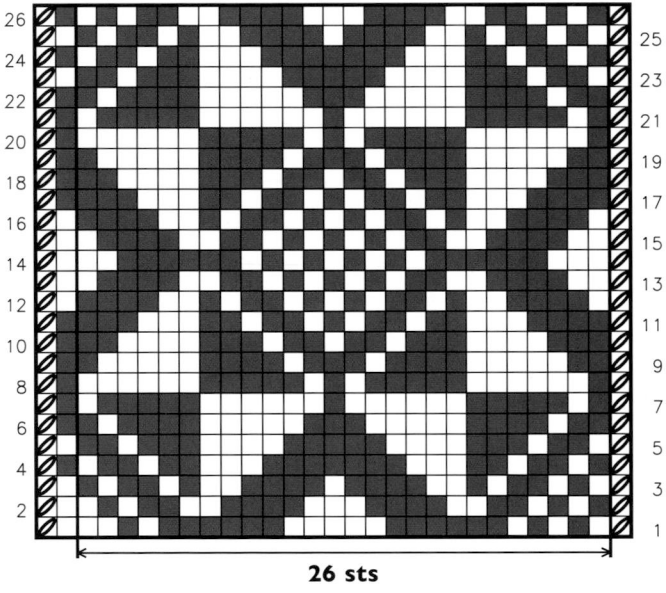

26 sts

Multiple of 26 sts + 1 + 2 edge sts

On right and wrong side rows, work in stockinette stitch in Jacquard technique according to the knitting pattern. On right side rows, repeat the pattern of 26 stitches following the edge stitch and end as drawn. Repeat rows 1–26.

Tip: Try knitting this pattern in only one color. In the swatch on the left, the white stitches are worked in reverse stockinette stitch and the blue stitches are worked in stockinette stitch. The result is a pattern with an interesting texture.

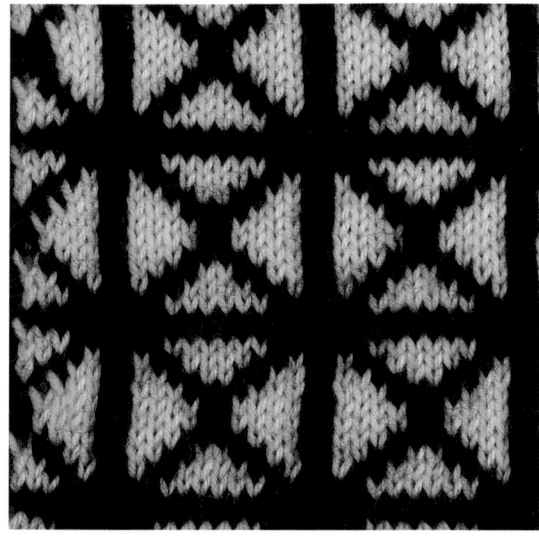

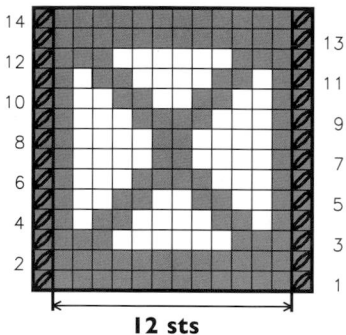

12 sts

Multiple of 12 sts + 2 edge sts

On right and wrong side rows, work in stockinette stitch in Jacquard technique according to the knitting pattern. Following the edge stitch, repeat the pattern of 12 stitches and then edge stitch. Following rows 1 and 2, repeat rows 3–14.

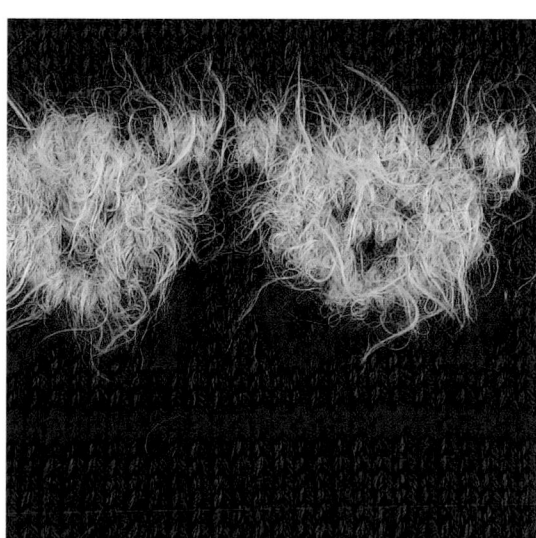

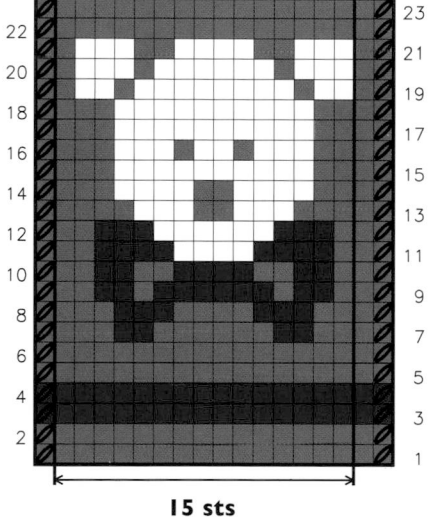

15 sts

Multiple of 15 sts + 1 + 2 edge sts

On right and wrong side rows, work in stockinette stitch in Jacquard technique according to the knitting pattern. Begin as indicated in the chart and repeat the pattern of 15 stitches and then edge stitch. Knit once rows 1–23.

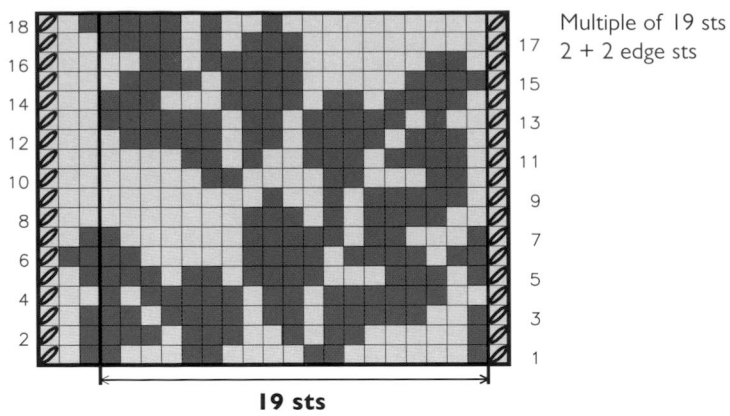

Multiple of 19 sts + 2 + 2 edge sts

19 sts

On right and wrong side rows, work in stockinette stitch in Jacquard technique according to the knitting pattern. Following the edge stitch, repeat the pattern of 19 stitches and end as drawn. Repeat rows 1–18.

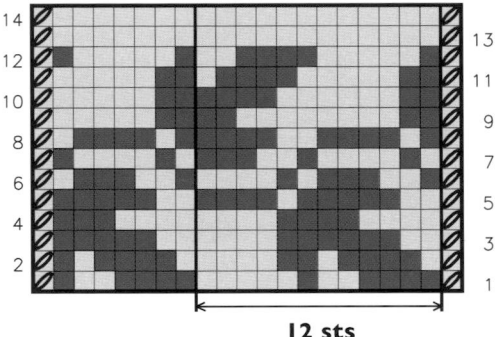

12 sts

Multiple of 12 sts + 7 + 2 edge sts

On right and wrong side rows, work in stockinette stitch in Jacquard technique according to the knitting pattern. On right side rows, following the edge stitch, repeat the pattern of 12 stitches and end as drawn. Repeat rows 1–14.

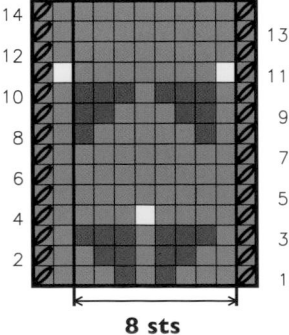

8 sts

Multiple of 8 sts + 1 + 2 edge sts

On right and wrong side rows, work in stockinette stitch in Jacquard technique according to the knitting pattern. On right side rows, following the edge stitch, repeat the pattern of 8 stitches and end as drawn. Repeat rows 1–14.

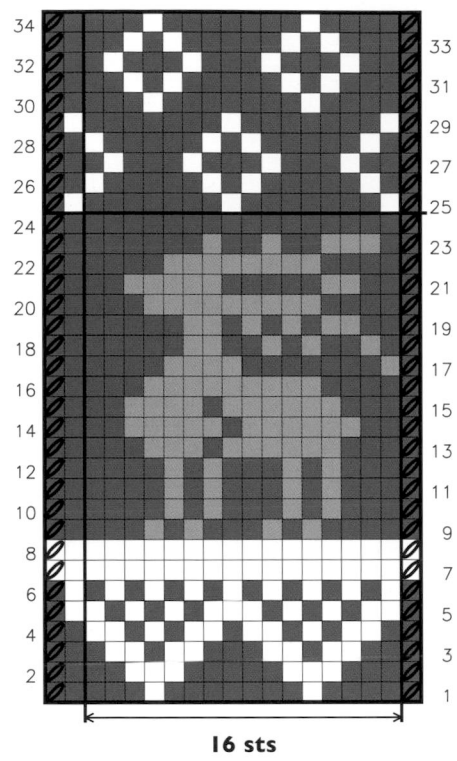

Multiple of 16 sts + 1 + 2 edge sts

On right and wrong side rows, work in stockinette stitch in Jacquard technique according to the knitting pattern. On right side rows, following the edge stitch, repeat the pattern of 16 stitches and end as drawn. Following rows 1–24, repeat rows 25–34.

16 sts

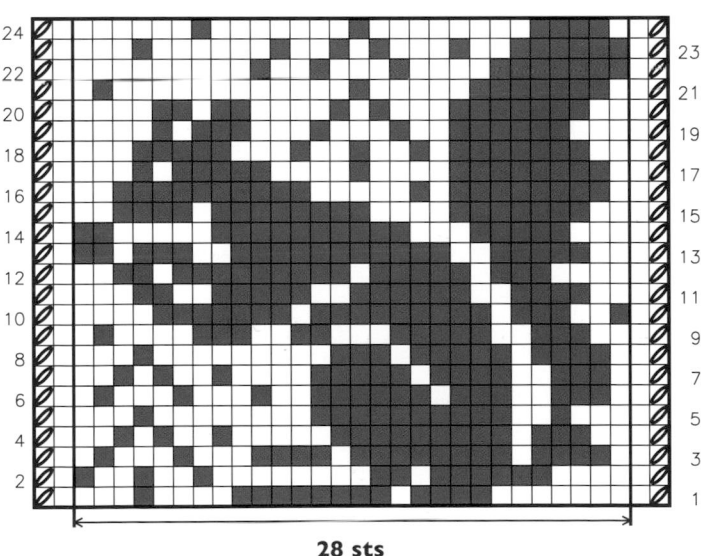

28 sts

Multiple of 28 sts + 2 + 2 edge sts

On right and wrong side rows, work in stockinette stitch in Jacquard technique according to the knitting pattern. Beginning as indicated in the chart, repeat the pattern of 28 stitches and end as drawn. Repeat rows 1–24.

Multiple of 32 sts + 1 + 2 edge sts

On right and wrong side rows, work in stockinette stitch in Jacquard technique according to the knitting pattern. On right side rows, following the edge stitch, repeat the pattern of 32 stitches and then edge stitch. Knit once rows 1–56.

32 sts

16 sts

Multiple of 16 sts + 1 + 2 edge sts

On right and wrong side rows, work in stockinette stitch in Jacquard technique according to the knitting pattern. On right side rows, following the edge stitch, begin as indicated in the chart and repeat the pattern of 16 stitches and then edge stitch. Repeat rows 1–24.

Multiple of 36 sts + 1 + 2 edge sts

On right and wrong side rows, work in stockinette stitch in Jacquard technique according to the knitting pattern. On right side rows, following the edge stitch, repeat the pattern of 36 stitches and then edge stitch. For the border, knit once rows 1–60. For the surface pattern, repeat rows 1–60.

36 sts

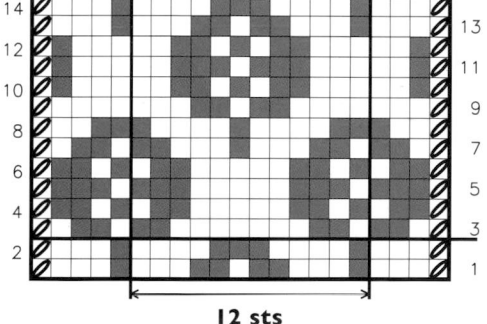

12 sts

Multiple of 12 sts + 7 + 2 edge sts

On right and wrong side rows, work in stockinette stitch in Jacquard technique according to the knitting pattern. Begin as indicated in the chart, repeat the pattern of 12 stitches and end as drawn. Following rows 1 and 2, repeat rows 3–14.

Jacquard Patterns

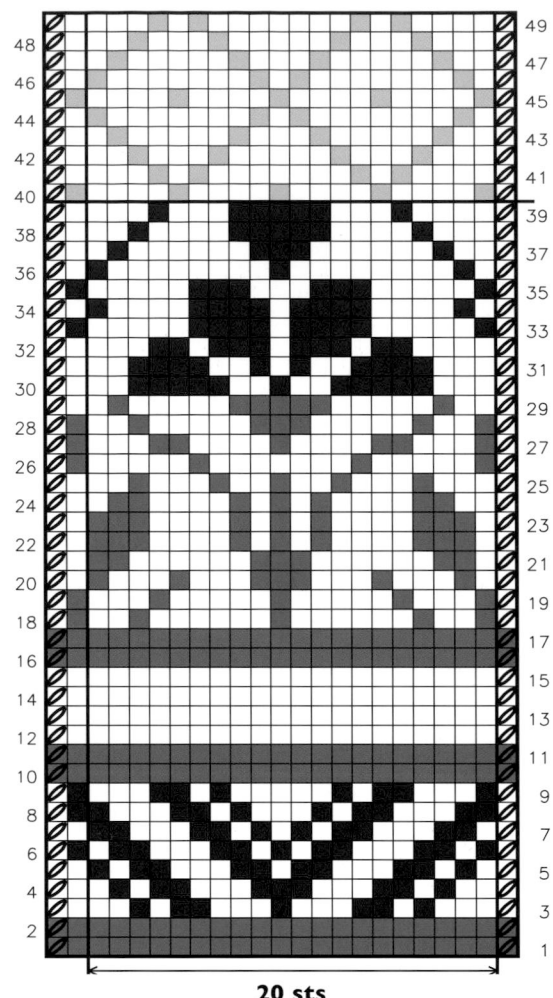

Multiple of 20 sts + 1 + 2 edge sts

On right and wrong side rows, work in stockinette stitch in Jacquard technique according to the knitting pattern. On right side rows, following the edge stitch, repeat the pattern of 20 stitches and end as drawn. Knit once rows 1–39, then repeat rows 40–49.

20 sts

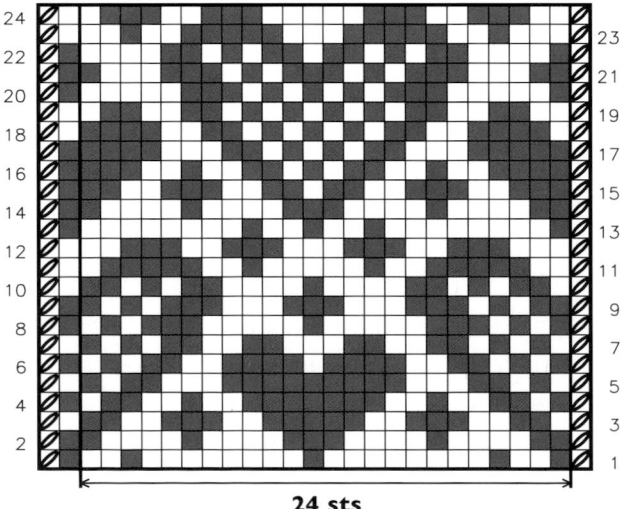

24 sts

Multiple of 24 sts + 1 + 2 edge sts

On right and wrong side rows, work in stockinette stitch in Jacquard technique according to the knitting pattern. On right side rows, following the edge stitch, repeat the pattern of 24 stitches and end as drawn. Repeat rows 1–24.

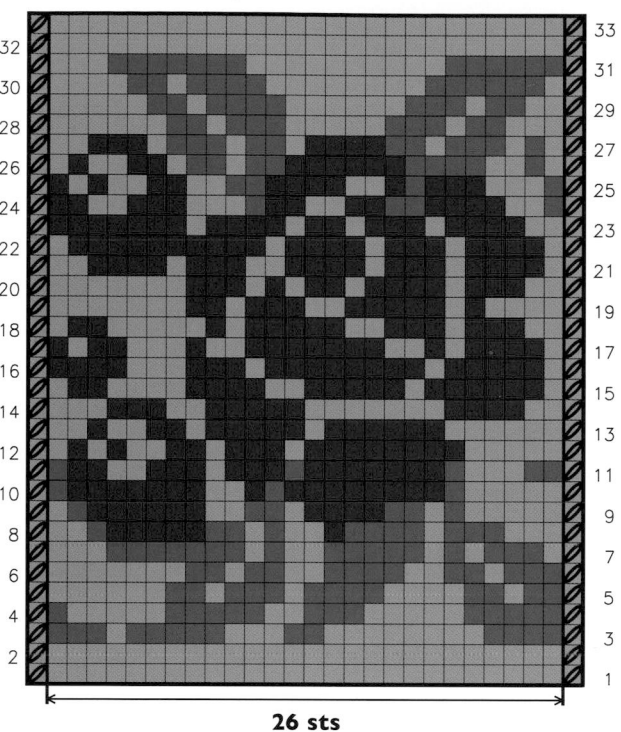

Multiple of 26 sts + 2 edge sts

On right and wrong side rows, work the border in stockinette stitch in Jacquard technique according to the knitting pattern. Following the edge stitch, repeat the pattern of 26 stitches and then edge stitch.
Knit once rows 1–33.

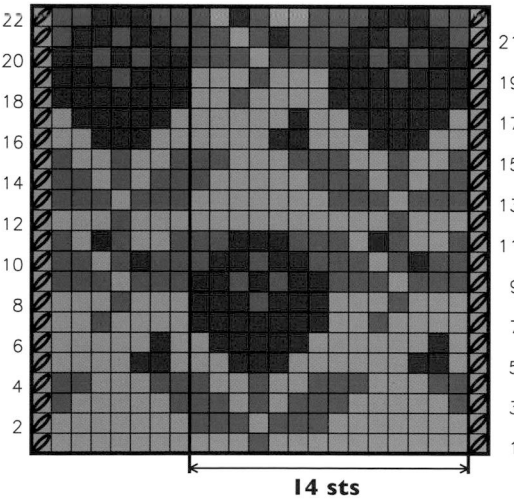

Multiple of 14 sts + 7 + 2 edge sts

On right and wrong side rows, work in stockinette stitch according to the knitting pattern. Following the edge stitch, repeat the pattern of 14 stitches on right side rows and end as drawn. Repeat rows 1–22.

Minipatterns

The small patterns in this section can be incorporated into all kinds of projects. They produce an even surface that can be used for an entire project or just as the background of a more elaborate piece. Because these pattern repeats encompass only a few rows and stitches, they are easy for beginning knitters to make.

These minipatterns should be done with smooth, single-color yarn. But you can also discover surprising designs by experimenting with different texture or multicolor yarns.

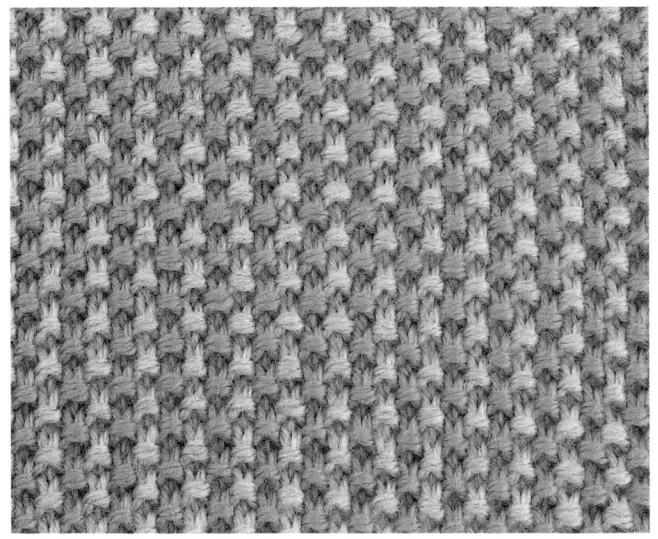

Cast on as many stitches as you like.

Row 1 (right side row): Purl all stitches.

Row 2 (wrong side row): Edge stitch, * make a loop: following stitch 1 on the left-hand needle insert your needle from the front to the back under the running thread between stitch 1 and 2 and draw the yarn through, then knit stitch 1; repeat from *, edge stitch.

Row 3: Purl the edge stitch together with the following stitch, * purl the loop together with the following stitch; repeat from *, purl the last loop, edge stitch.

Following row 1, repeat rows 2 and 3.

Multiple of 3 sts + 1 + 2 edge sts

Row 1 (right side row), lime green: Edge stitch, * make 1 knot: knit into the back of 3 stitches together twisted, but leave the stitches on the needle; make 1 yarn over and once again knit 3 stitches together twisted; then slip stitches off the needle; repeat from *, end with 1 knit stitch, edge stitch.

Row 2, lime green: Purl all stitches.

Row 3, camel: Edge stitch, knit 2 stitches, * make 1 knot; repeat from *; end with 2 knit stitches, edge stitch.

Row 4, camel: Purl all stitches.

Row 5, beige: Edge stitch, knit 1 stitch, * make 1 knot; repeat from *, edge stitch.

Row 6, beige: Purl all stitches.

Repeat rows 1–6.

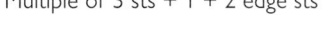

Multiple of 3 sts + 1 + 2 edge sts

Row 1 (wrong side row): Edge stitch, knit 1 stitch, * 1 yarn over, purl 2 stitches together, 1 knit stitch; repeat from *, edge stitch.

Row 2 (right side row): Edge stitch, purl 1 stitch, * 1 yarn over, knit 1 stitch together with the following yarn over by knitting into back of stitch, purl 1 stitch; repeat from *, edge stitch.

Row 3: Edge stitch, knit 1 stitch, * 1 yarn over, purl the following stitch together with the yarn over, knit 1 stitch; repeat from *, edge stitch.

Following rows 1, repeat rows 2 and 3.

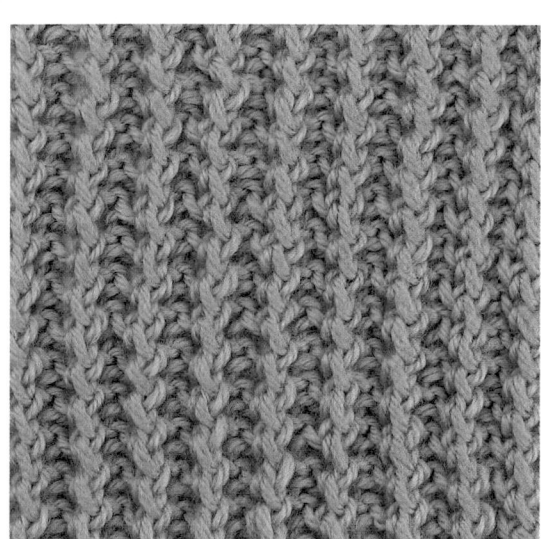

Even number of stitches

Row 1 (wrong side row): Edge stitch, * purl 1 stitch, with yarn in front slip 1 stitch purlwise, make 1 yarn over; repeat from *, edge stitch.

Row 2 (right side row): Edge stitch, * knit the following stitch together with the yarn over, 1 knit stitch; repeat from *, edge stitch.

Row 3: Edge stitch, * with yarn in front slip 1 stitch purlwise, make 1 yarn over, purl 1 stitch; repeat from *, edge stitch.

Row 4: Edge stitch, * knit 1 stitch, knit the following stitch together with the yarn over; repeat from *, edge stitch.

Repeat rows 1–4.

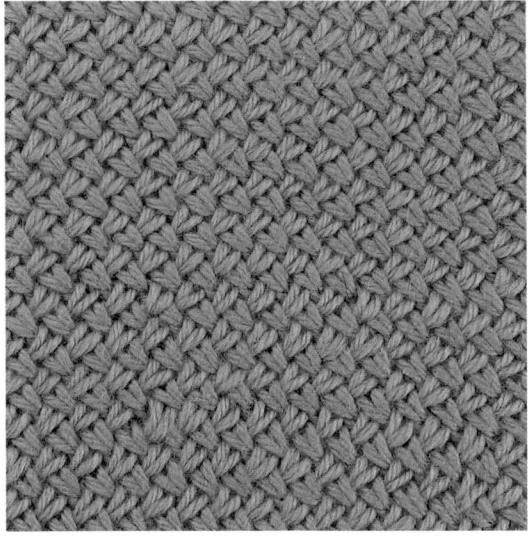

Even number of stitches

Row 1 (right side row): Edge stitch, knit 1 stitch, * knit into back of stitch 2 on the left-hand needle by passing the right-hand needle behind stitch 1, then knit stitch 1 and let both stitches slide off the left-hand needle; repeat from *, end with 1 knit stitch, edge stitch.

Row 2: Edge stitch, * first purl stitch 2 of the left-hand needle by passing the right-hand needle in front of stitch 1, then purl stitch 1 and let both stitches slide off the left-hand needle; repeat from *, edge stitch.

Repeat rows 1 and 2.

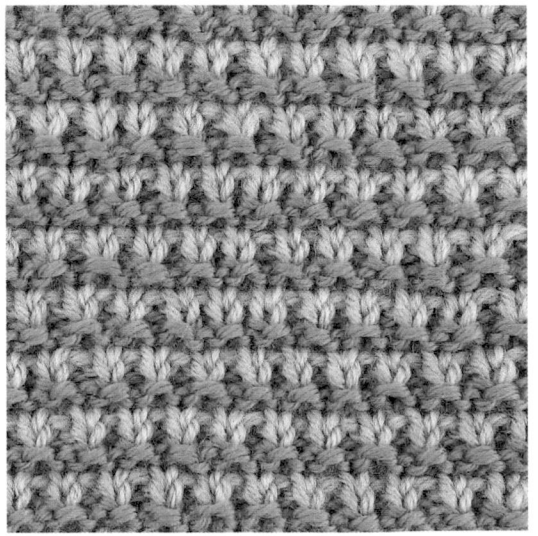

Odd number of stitches

Row 1 (wrong side row), lime green: Knit all stitches.

Row 2 (right side row), camel: Edge stitch, alternately purl 1 stitch and then knit 1 stitch, end with 1 purl stitch, edge stitch.

Row 3, camel: Work stitches in rib pattern.

Row 4 and 5, lime green: Work 1 garter rib; knit both rows.

Row 6, camel: Edge stitch, alternately knit 1 stitch and then purl 1 stitch, end with 1 knit stitch, edge stitch.

Row 7, camel: Work stitches in rib pattern.

Rows 8 and 9, lime green: Work 1 garter rib.

Following row 1, repeat rows 2–9.

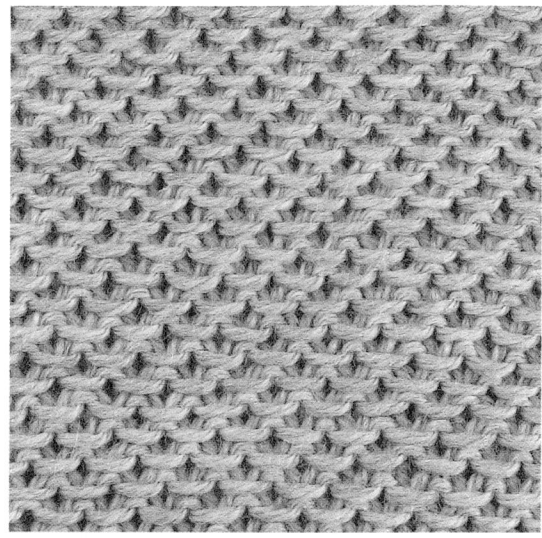

Even number of stitches

Row 1 (right side row): Edge stitch, * slip 1 stitch purlwise with yarn in front of stitch, 1 purl stitch; repeat from *, edge stitch.

Row 2: Purl all stitches.

Row 3: Edge stitch, * purl 1 stitch, slip 1 stitch purlwise with yarn in front of stitch; repeat from *, edge stitch.

Row 4: Purl all stitches.

Repeat rows 1–4.

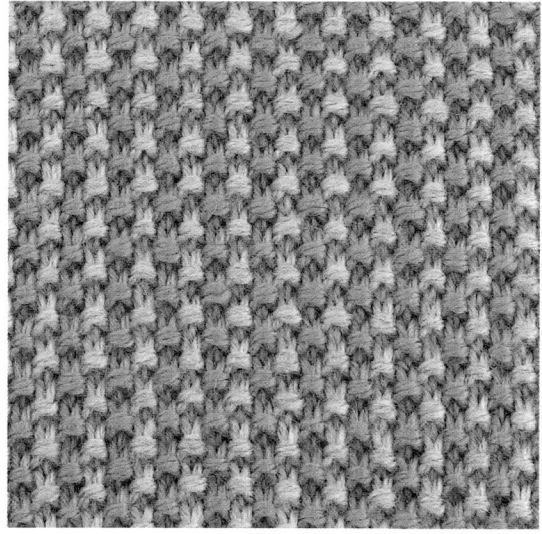

Odd number of stitches

Tip: Knit this pattern loosely.

Row 1 (wrong side row), beige: Edge stitch, alternately knit 1 stitch and then purl 1 stitch, ending with 1 knit stitch, edge stitch.

Row 2 (right side row), lime green: Edge stitch, * slip 1 stitch purlwise with yarn in back of stitch, knit 1 stitch; repeat from *, end with slipping 1 stitch purlwise with yarn in back of stitch, edge stitch.

Row 3, lime green: Edge stitch, slip 1 stitch purlwise with yarn in front of stitch, * knit 1 stitch, slip 1 stitch purlwise with yarn in front of stitch; repeat from *, edge stitch.

Row 4, beige: Edge stitch, * knit 1 stitch, slip 1 stitch purlwise with yarn in back of stitch; repeat from *, end with 1 knit stitch, edge stitch.

Row 5, beige: Edge stitch, knit 1 stitch, * slip 1 stitch purlwise with yarn in front of stitch, knit 1 stitch; repeat from *, edge stitch.

Following row 1, repeat rows 2–5.

Even number of stitches

Row 1 (right side row): Edge stitch, * knit into back of stitch, purl into back of stitch; repeat from *, edge stitch.

Row 2: Knit all stitches.

Repeat rows 1 and 2.

Multiple of 4 sts + 3 + 2 edge sts

Row 1 (right side row): Edge stitch, knit 1 stitch, * purl 1 stitch, knit 3 stitches; repeat from *, end with 1 purl stitch, 1 knit stitch, edge stitch.

Row 2: Purl all stitches.

Row 3: Edge stitch, knit 3 stitches, * purl 1 stitch, knit 3 stitches; repeat from *, edge stitch.

Row 4: Purl all stitches.

Repeat rows 1–4.

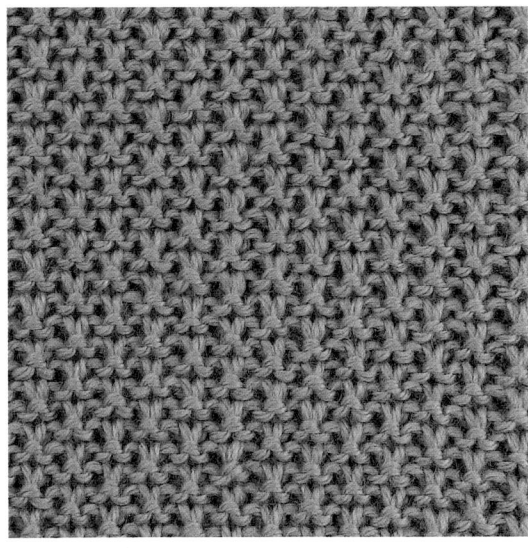

Multiple of 4 sts + 3 + 2 edge sts

Row 1 (right side row): Edge stitch, * knit 3 stitches, slip 1 stitch purlwise with yarn in back of stitch; repeat from *, knit 3 stitches, edge stitch.

Row 2: * Knit 3 stitches, slip 1 stitch purlwise with yarn in front of stitch; repeat from *, knit 3 stitches, edge stitch.

Row 3: Edge stitch, knit 1 stitch, * slip 1 stitch purlwise with yarn in back of stitch, knit 3 stitches; repeat from *, slip 1 stitch purlwise with yarn in back of stitch, knit 1 stitch, edge stitch.

Row 4: Edge stitch, knit 1 stitch, * slip 1 stitch purlwise with yarn in front of stitch, knit 3 stitches; repeat from *, slip 1 stitch purlwise with yarn in front of stitch, knit 1 stitch, edge stitch.

Repeat rows 1–4.

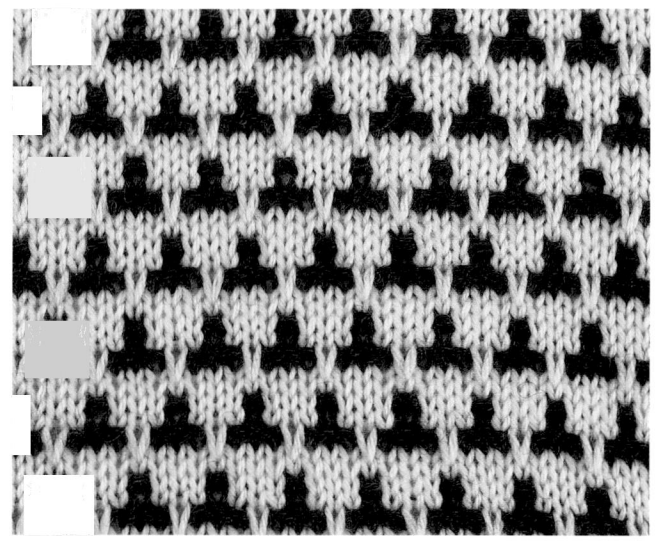

Slip-Stitch Patterns

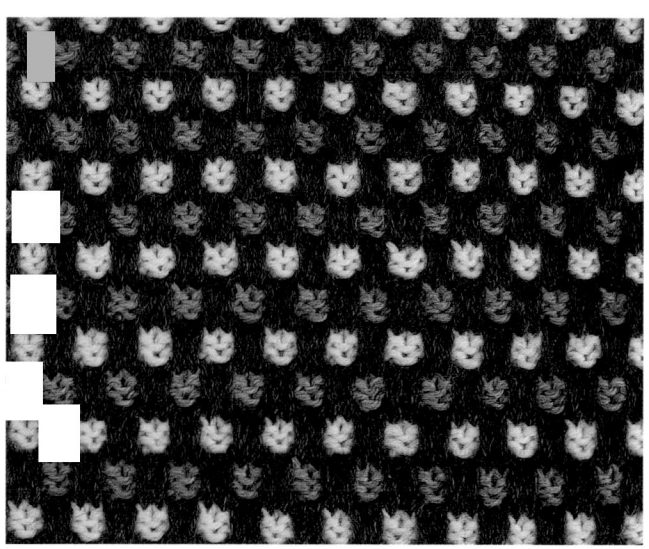

It is hard to believe that only a single-color yarn is knitted into each row of these multicolor and intricate patterns. These long strips, checks, geometric designs, and even flowers, which appear to have been done using the Jacquard technique, are created by slipping certain stitches and then knitting them first in one of the following rows once more.

Be creative in your choice of yarn when working with these patterns: Combine smooth with bulky yarns or monochromatic with multicolor yarns. But keep in mind that these patterns use up more yarn. Because of the slip stitches, you will need more rows or rounds for a 4-inch (10-cm) swatch than normal.

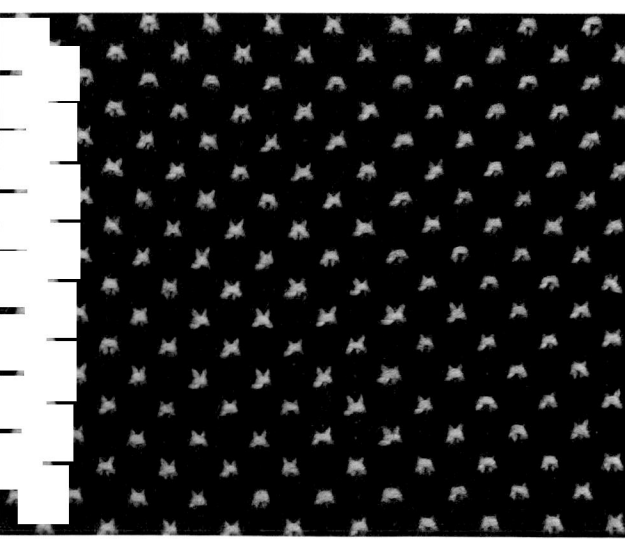

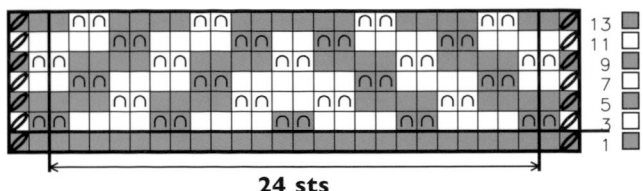

24 sts

Multiple of 24 sts + 2 + 2 edge sts

On right side rows, work according to the knitting chart. Beginning as indicated in the chart, repeat the pattern of 24 stitches and end as drawn. On wrong side rows, purl all stitches, slipping the slipped stitches of the right side rows with yarn in front of work. Following rows 1 and 2, repeat rows 3–14.

The small boxes next to the row numbers indicate with which color the rows are knitted.

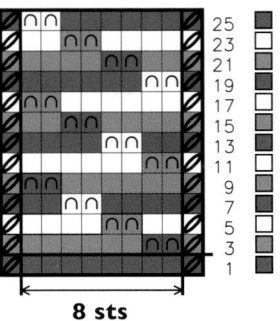

8 sts

Multiple of 8 sts + 2 edge sts

On right side rows, work according to the knitting chart. Following the edge stitch, repeat the pattern of 8 stitches and then edge stitch. On wrong side rows, purl all stitches, slipping the slipped stitches of the right side rows purlwise with yarn in front of work. Following rows 1 and 2, repeat rows 3–26.

The small boxes next to the row numbers indicate with which color the rows are knitted.

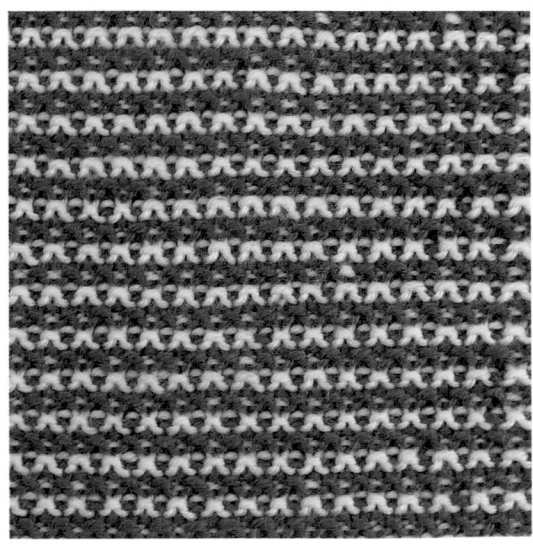

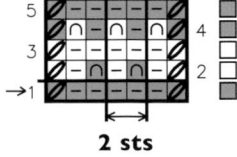

2 sts

Multiple of 2 sts + 1 + 2 edge sts

The pattern begins with a wrong side row. On right and wrong side rows, work according to the knitting chart. Begin as indicated in the chart, repeat the pattern of 2 stitches, and end as drawn. Following row 1, repeat rows 2–5.

The small boxes next to the row numbers indicate with which color the rows are knitted.

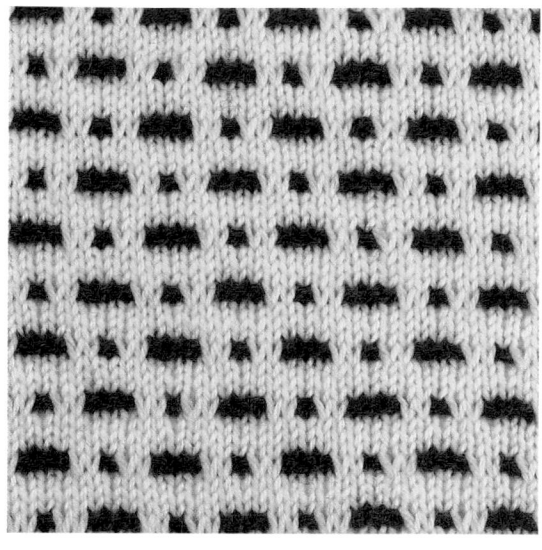

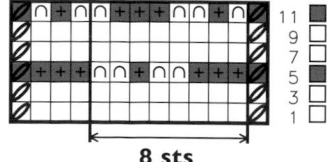

8 sts

Multiple of 8 sts + 3 + 2 edge sts

On right side rows, work according to the knitting chart. Following the edge stitch, repeat the pattern of 8 stitches and end as drawn. On wrong side rows, work stitches in pattern or as explained in the description of the symbols, slipping the slipped stitches of the right side rows with yarn in front of work. Repeat rows 1–12.

The small boxes next to the row numbers indicate with which color the rows are knitted.

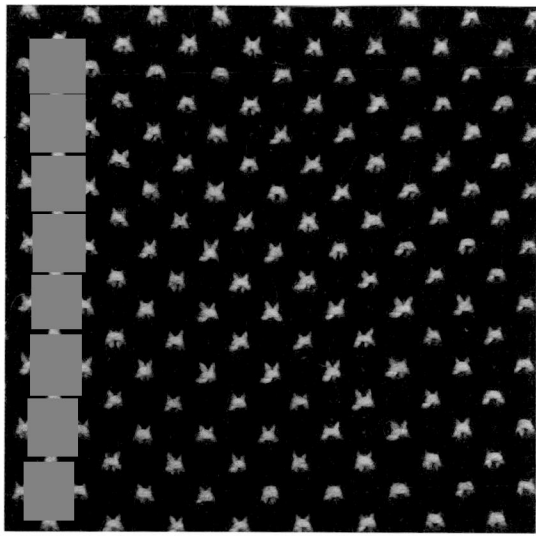

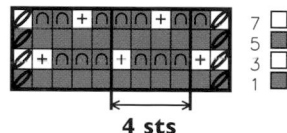

4 sts

Multiple of 4 sts + 1 + 2 edge sts

On right side rows, work according to the knitting chart. Beginning as indicated in the chart, repeat the pattern of 4 stitches and end as drawn. On wrong side rows, work stitches in pattern, slipping the slipped stitches of the right side rows purlwise with yarn in front of work. Repeat rows 1–8.

The small boxes next to the row numbers indicate with which color the rows are knitted.

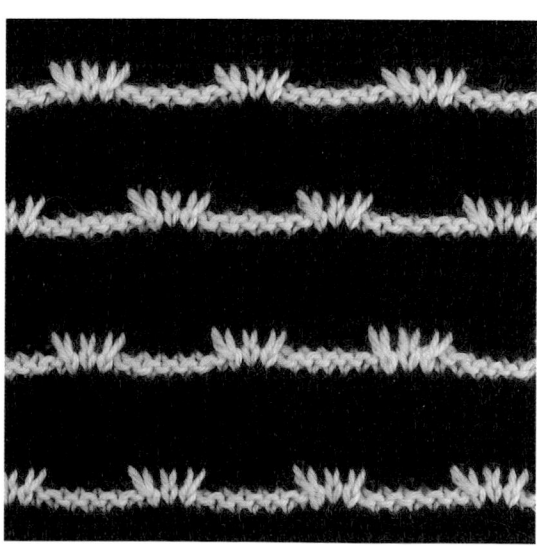

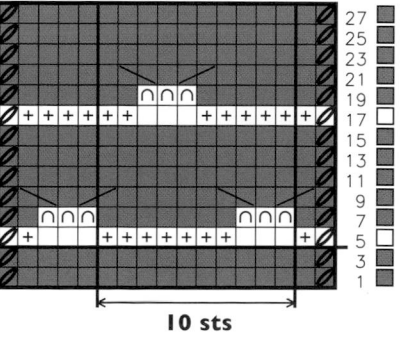

10 sts

Multiple of 10 sts + 5 + 2 edge sts

On right side rows, work according to the knitting chart. Beginning as indicated in the chart, repeat the pattern of 10 stitches and end as drawn. On wrong side rows, work stitches in pattern or as explained in the description of the symbols, slipping the slipped stitches of the right side rows with yarn in front of work. Following rows 1–4, repeat rows 5–28.

The small boxes next to the row numbers indicate with which color the rows are knitted.

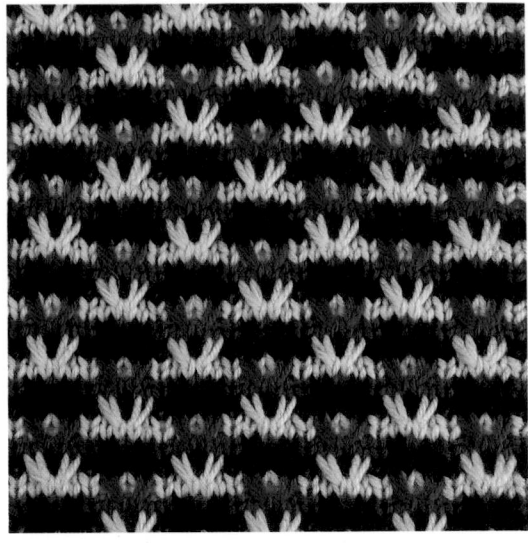

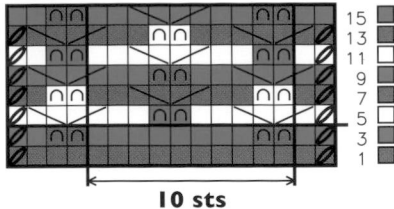

10 sts

Multiple of 10 sts + 4 + 2 edge sts

On right side rows, work according to the knitting chart. Beginning as indicated in the chart, repeat the pattern of 10 stitches and end as drawn. On wrong side rows, purl all stitches, slipping the slipped stitches of the right side rows with yarn in front of work. Following rows 1–4, repeat rows 5–16.

The small boxes next to the row numbers indicate with which color the rows are knitted.

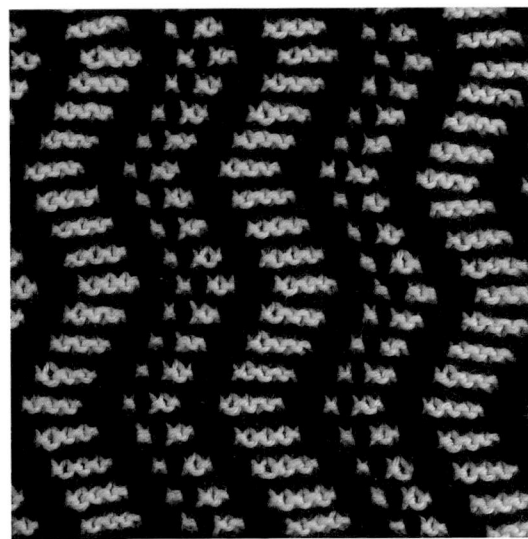

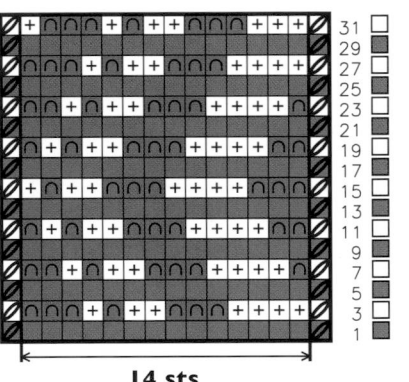

14 sts

Multiple of 14 sts + 2 edge sts

On right side rows, work according to the knitting chart. Following the edge stitch, repeat the pattern of 14 stitches and then edge stitch. On wrong side rows, knit all stitches in pattern or as explained in the description of the symbols, slipping the slipped stitches of the right side rows with yarn in front of stitch. Repeat rows 1–32.

The small boxes next to the row numbers indicate with which color the rows are knitted.

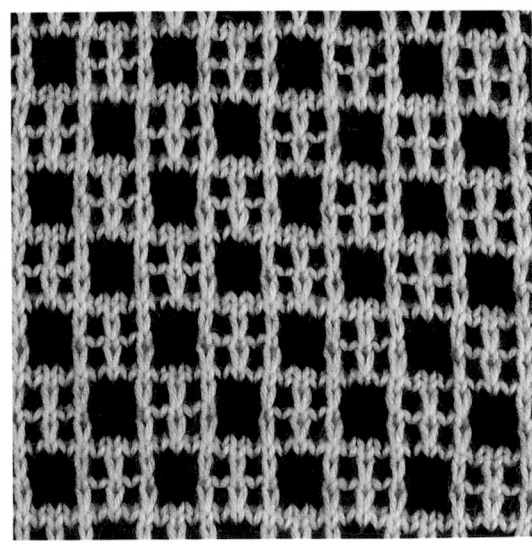

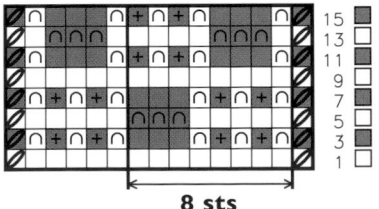

8 sts

Multiple of 8 sts + 5 + 2 edge sts

On right side rows, work according to the knitting chart. Following the edge stitch, repeat the pattern of 8 stitches and end as drawn. On wrong side rows, work stitches in pattern or as explained in the description of the symbols, slipping the slipped stitches of the right side rows with yarn in front of work. Repeat rows 1–16.

The small boxes next to the row numbers indicate with which color the rows are knitted.

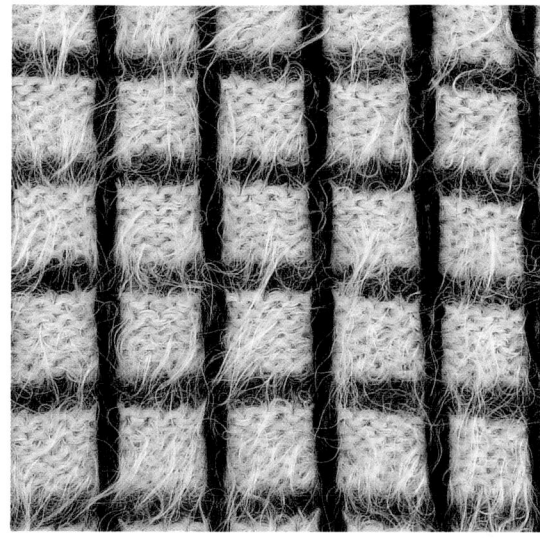

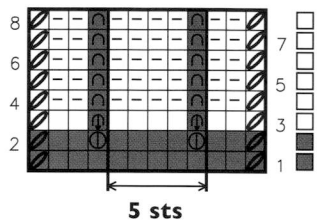

5 sts

Multiple of 5 sts + 2 edge sts

On right and wrong side rows, work according to the knitting chart. Beginning as indicated in the chart, repeat the pattern of 5 stitches and end as drawn. On wrong side rows, the yarn is in front of work with slipped stitches. Repeat rows 1–8.

The small boxes next to the row numbers indicate with which color the rows are knitted.

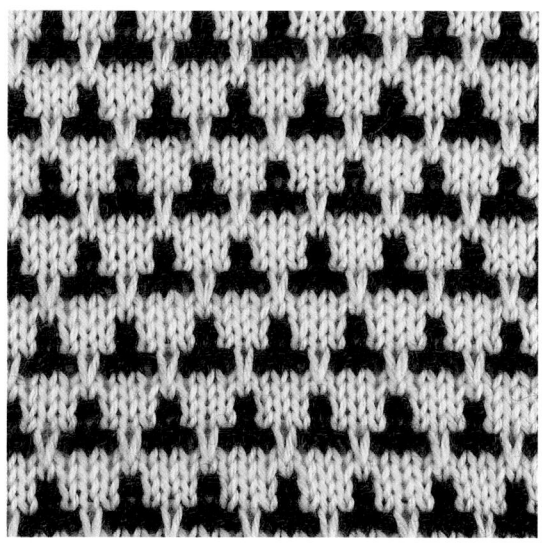

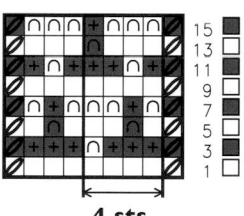

4 sts

Multiple of 4 sts + 3 + 2 edge sts

On right side rows, work according to the knitting chart. Following the edge stitch, repeat the pattern of 4 stitches and end as drawn. On wrong side rows, work stitches in pattern or as explained in the description of the symbols, slipping the slipped stitches of the right side rows purlwise with yarn in front of work. Repeat rows 1–16.

The small boxes next to the row numbers indicate with which color the rows are knitted.

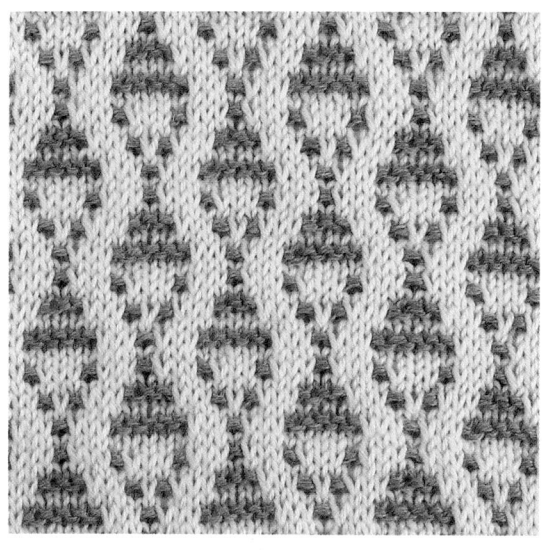

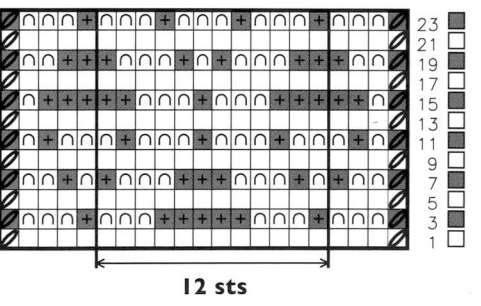

12 sts

Multiple of 12 sts + 7 + 2 edge sts

On right side rows, work according to the knitting chart. Beginning as indicated in the chart, repeat the pattern of 12 stitches and end as drawn. On wrong side rows, work stitches in pattern or as explained in the description of the symbols, slipping the slipped stitches of the right side rows with yarn in front of work. Repeat rows 1–24.

The small boxes next to the row numbers indicate with which color the rows are knitted.

Slip-Stitch Patterns

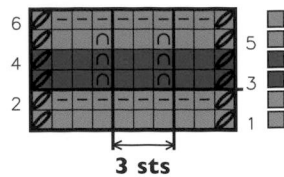

3 sts

Multiple of 3 sts + 2 + 2 edge sts

On right and wrong side rows, work according to the knitting chart. Beginning as indicated in the chart, repeat the pattern of 3 stitches and end as drawn. On right side rows, slip the slipped stitches with yarn in back of work. On wrong side rows, slip the slipped stitches with yarn in front of work. Following rows 1 and 2, repeat rows 3–6.

The small boxes next to the row numbers indicate with which color the rows are knitted.

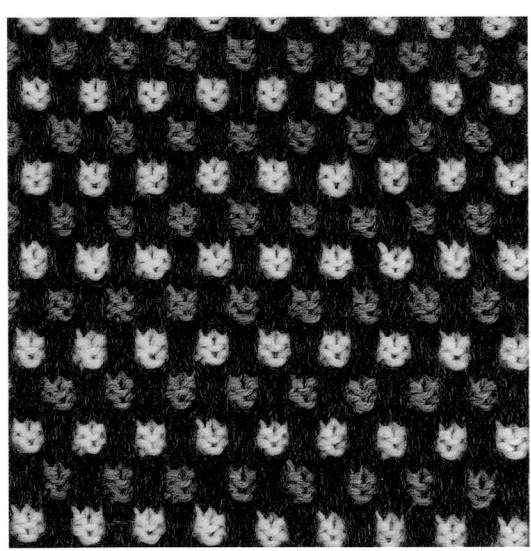

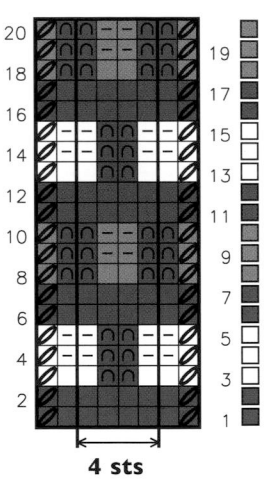

4 sts

Multiple of 4 sts + 2 + 2 edge sts

On right and wrong side rows, work according to the knitting chart. Beginning as indicated in the chart, repeat the pattern of 4 stitches and end as drawn. On right side rows, slip the slipped stitches with yarn in back of work. On wrong side rows, slip the slipped stitches with yarn in front of work. Repeat rows 1–20.

The small boxes next to the row numbers indicate with which color the rows are knitted.

Hint: Work this pattern with a circular needle so that the stitches can be pushed at the end of the needle with the necessary yarn.

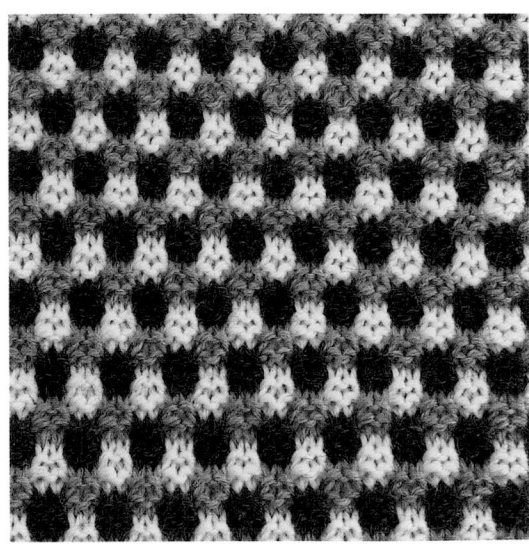

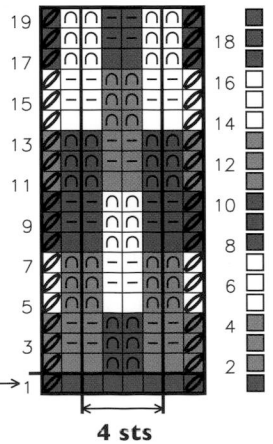

4 sts

Multiple of 4 sts + 2 + 2 edge sts

The pattern begins with a wrong side row. On right and wrong side rows, work according to the knitting chart. Beginning as indicated in the chart, repeat the pattern of 4 stitches and end as drawn. On right side rows, slip the slipped stitches with yarn in back of work. On wrong side rows, slip the slipped stitches with yarn in front of work. Following row 1, repeat rows 2–19.

The small boxes next to the row numbers indicate with which color the rows are knitted.

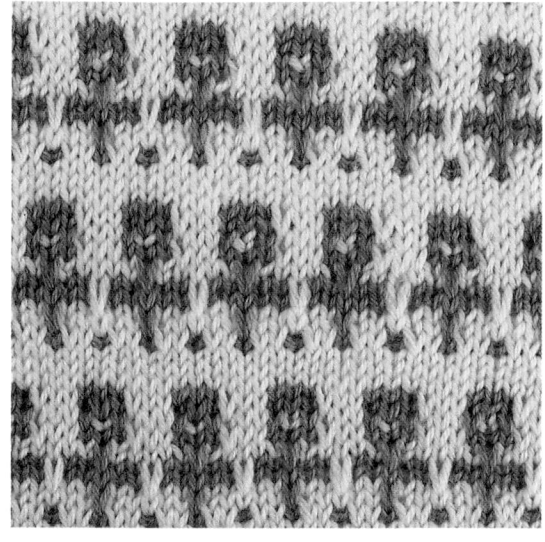

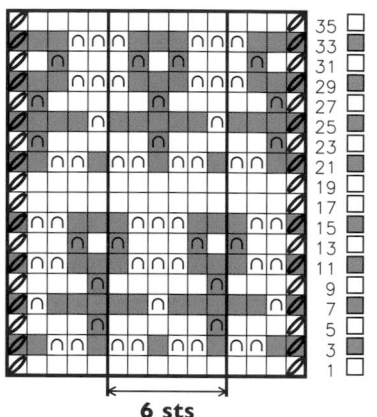

Multiple of 6 sts + 1 + 2 edge sts

On right side rows, work according to the knitting chart. Beginning as indicated in the chart, repeat the pattern of 6 stitches and end as drawn. On wrong side rows, purl all stitches, slipping the slipped stitches of the right side rows purlwise with yarn in front of work. Repeat rows 1–36.

6 sts

The small boxes next to the row numbers indicate with which color the rows are knitted.

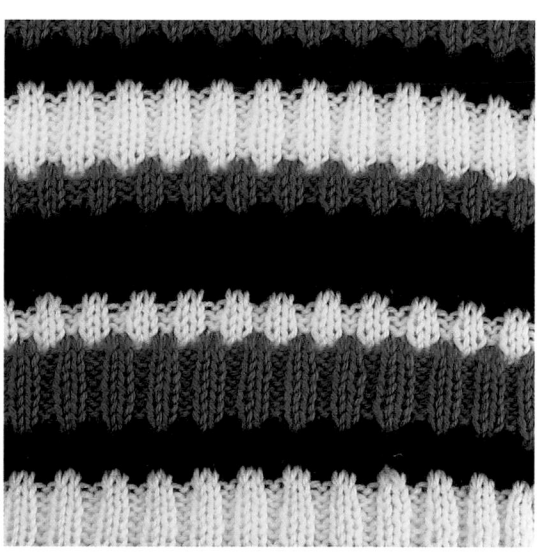

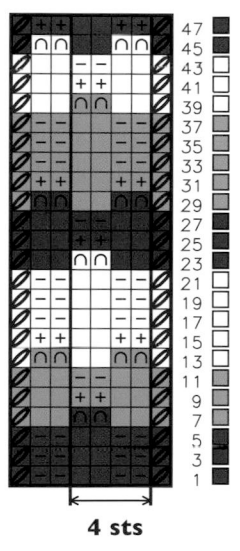

Multiple of 4 sts + 2 + 2 edge sts

On right side rows, work according to the knitting chart. Following the edge stitch, repeat the pattern of 4 stitches and end as drawn. On wrong side rows, work stitches in pattern or as explained in the description of the symbols, slipping the slipped stitches of the right side rows purlwise with yarn in front of work. Repeat rows 1–48.

4 sts

The small boxes next to the row numbers indicate with which color the rows are knitted.

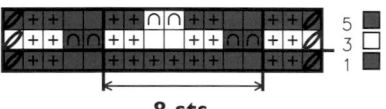

8 sts

Multiple of 8 sts + 6 + 2 edge sts

On right side rows, work according to the knitting chart. Beginning as indicated in the chart, repeat the pattern of 8 stitches and end as drawn. On wrong side rows, work stitches in pattern or as explained in the description of the symbols, slipping the slipped stitches of the right side rows purlwise with yarn in front of work. Following rows 1 and 2, repeat rows 3–6.

The small boxes next to the row numbers indicate with which color the rows are knitted.

Knitting into Stitches Below Patterns

What is usually considered a knitting mistake is a technique with the patterns in this section: Instead of knitting into the next stitch on the left-hand needle, you insert your needle one or more rows down and knit this stitch. In the rows above it, this stitch will come undone by itself. If you stagger the arrangement of knitting into stitches below, you will get an interesting honeycomb design.

This technique can be worked with many variations. For example, you can slip one, or several, stitches instead of knitting them and carry the working yarn loosely along at the front of the work. After several rows knitted in this manner, you can then bring together the floats with a loop.

For lace patterns, this technique can also be used effectively by drawing a loop through each small hole. Extra stitches that are made can be decreased by knitting them together. For slip-stitch patterns (see page 87), you can experiment with different colors and types of yarn. They can be worked with monochromatic or multicolor, smooth or textured.

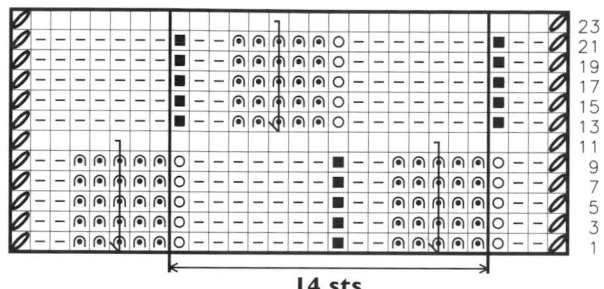

14 sts

Multiple of 14 sts + 9 + 2 edge sts

On right side rows, work according to the knitting chart. Beginning as indicated in the chart, repeat the pattern of 14 stitches and end as drawn. On wrong side rows, purl all stitches and drop the yarn overs of the right side rows. Repeat rows 1–24.

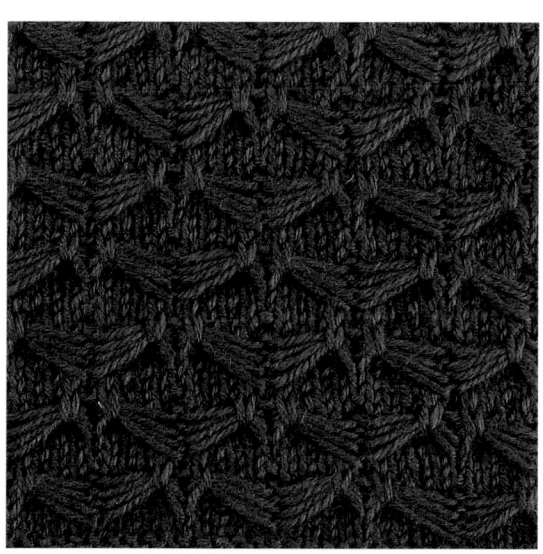

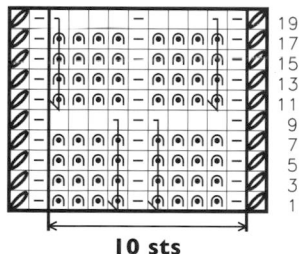

10 sts

Multiple of 10 sts + 1 + 2 edge sts

On right side rows, work according to the knitting chart. Following the edge stitch, repeat the pattern of 10 stitches and end as drawn. With slipped stitches, loosely carry the yarn in front of stitches. On wrong side rows, purl all stitches. Repeat rows 1–20.

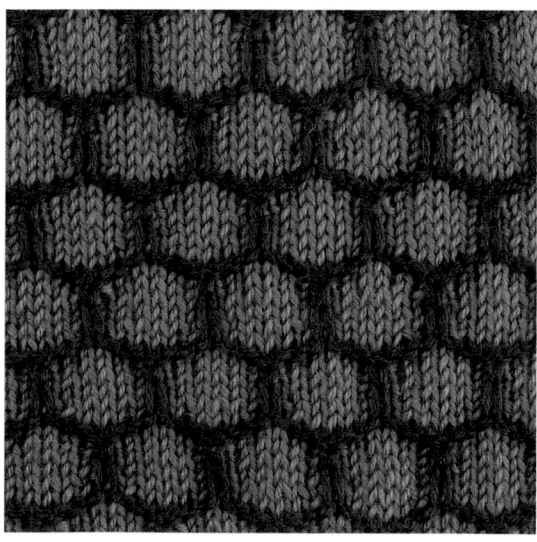

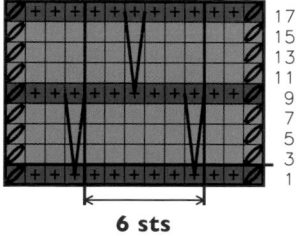

6 sts

Multiple of 6 sts + 5 + 2 edge sts

On right side rows, work according to the knitting chart. Beginning as indicated in the chart, repeat the pattern of 6 stitches and end as drawn. On wrong side rows, work stitches in pattern or as explained in the description of the symbols. Following rows 1 and 2, repeat rows 3–18.

 = With the left-hand needle, take up the above-lying running thread from the purl stitch of the garter rib lying below by inserting your needle from top to bottom; then work together the running thread and the 1st stitch of the left-hand needle by knitting into the back of the stitch.

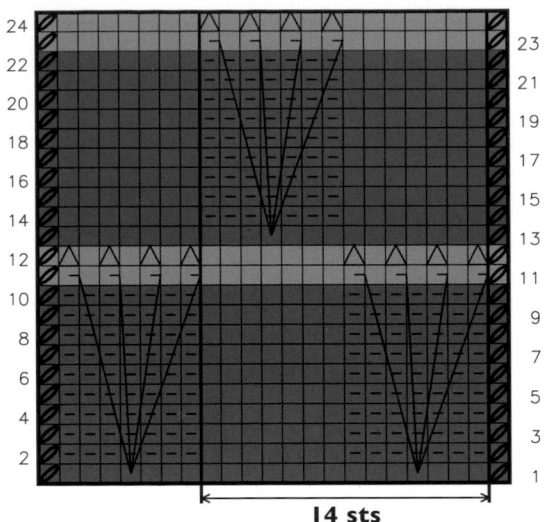

Multiple of 14 sts + 7 + 2 edge sts

On right and wrong side rows, work according to the knitting chart. Following the edge stitch, repeat the pattern of 14 stitches and end as drawn. Repeat rows 1–24.

 = Knit the 1st stitch of the reverse stockinette check; with the right-hand needle, pull a loop through the stitch, which is marked by the lower pointed edge of the sign and stretch it, * knit 2 stitches, pick 1 loop as before; repeat twice from *.

 = On the following wrong side row, purl stitch and loop together.

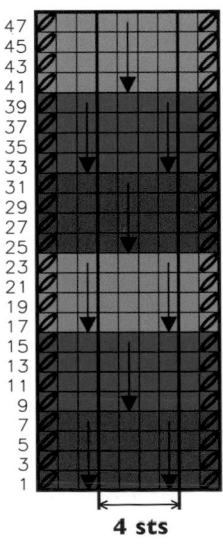

Multiple of 4 sts + 3 + 2 edge sts

In this pattern, the 1st row and each following odd row is a wrong side row. Therefore, purl all stitches.

Work according to the knitting chart. Beginning as indicated in the chart, repeat the pattern of 4 stitches and end as drawn. On right side rows, knit all stitches or as indicated in the chart. Repeat rows 1–48.

 = In each last row (right side row) of the color strips, insert your right-hand needle into the corresponding stitch of row 1 of the color strip and draw through 1 loop, then slip the corresponding stitch off the left-hand needle and undo it.

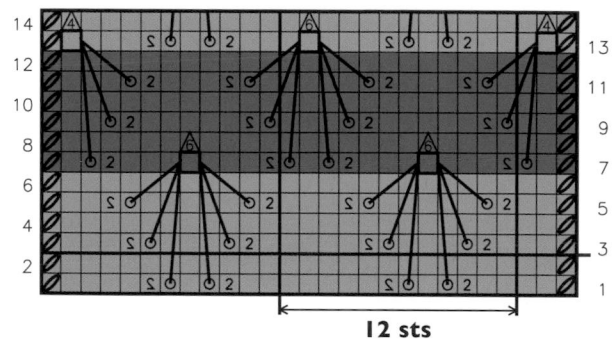

12 sts

Multiple of 12 sts + 1 + 2 edge sts

On right and wrong side rows, work according to the knitting chart. Beginning as indicated in the chart, repeat the pattern of 12 stitches and end as drawn. Following rows 1 and 2, repeat rows 3–14.

 = Knit up to the circled stitch, then draw 1 loop through the upper-right hole by inserting your right-hand needle from the front to the back; draw 1 loop each through the following 2 holes as well, knitting the circled stitches and draw 1 loop each through the following 3 holes beginning with the lower hole.

 = At the beginning of the row, knit circled stitch, drawing 1 loop each through the following 3 holes beginning with the hole at the bottom.

 = At the end of the row, knit up to the circled stitch; beginning with the upper hole, draw 1 loop through each hole, then knit the circled stitch.

 = In the following wrong side row, purl the corresponding stitch together with the corresponding 3 or 6 loops.

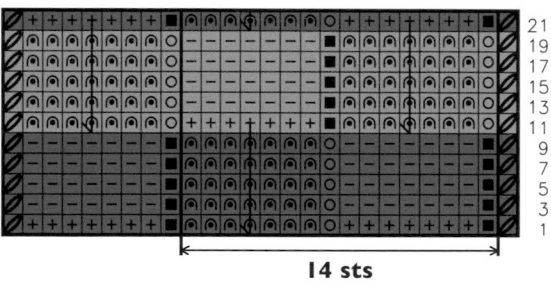

14 sts

Multiple of 14 sts + 7 + 2 edge sts

On right side rows, work according to the knitting chart. Following the edge stitch, repeat the pattern of 14 stitches and end as drawn. On wrong side rows, work stitches in pattern or as explained in the description of the symbols; purl the slipped stitches of the right side rows and drop the yarn overs. Following rows 1 and 2, repeat rows 3–22.

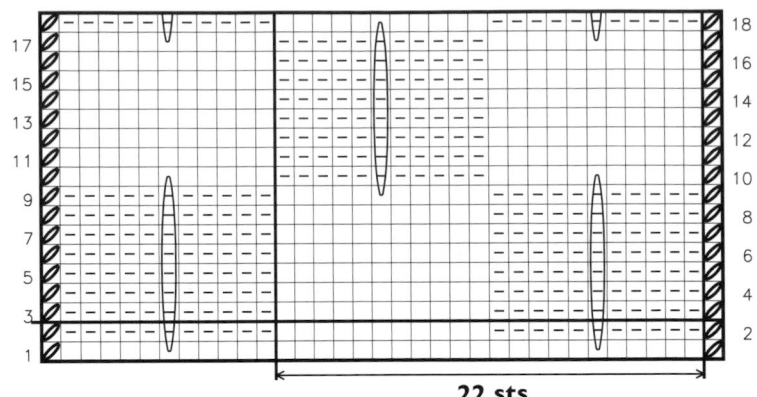

22 sts

Multiple of 22 sts + 11 + 2 edge sts

The pattern starts with a wrong side row. On right and wrong side rows, work according to the knitting chart. Begin row 1 as indicated in the chart, repeat the pattern of 22 stitches and then edge stitch. Following rows 1 and 2, repeat rows 3–18.

= Knit up to the middle stitch of the reverse stockinette check. With the right-hand needle, draw 1 loop through the middle stitch of the last row of the stockinette check below; lift the loop onto the left-hand needle and work the loop together with the following stitch by knitting into the back of the stitch.

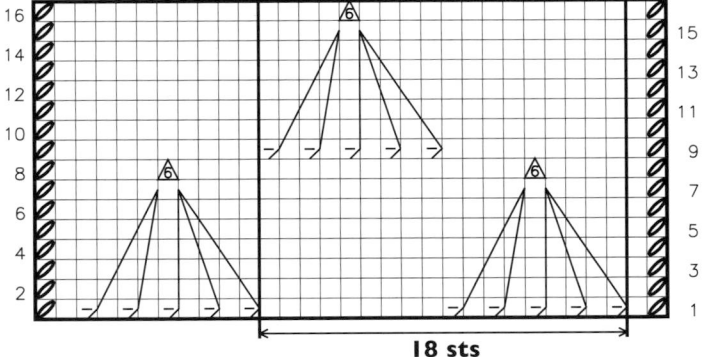

18 sts

Multiple of 18 sts + 11 + 2 edge sts

On right and wrong side rows, work according to the knitting chart. Beginning as indicated in the chart, repeat the pattern of 18 stitches and end as drawn. Repeat rows 1–16.

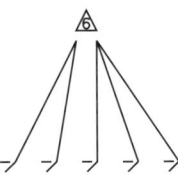

= Knit up to the corresponding stitch, then knit with the right-hand needle from the front to the back under the 1st purled stitch and draw through 1 loop; stretch the latter; under the following 2 purled stitches draw 1 loop each, knit the stitch; under the 2 remaining purled stitches draw 1 loop each. Purl together the 5 loops and the stitch on the following wrong side row.

Patterns from the Alpine Region

The variety of traditional knitting patterns from the Alpine region is simply inexhaustible. Knitters there add their own signature in decorating traditional stockings, cardigans, and vests. As a result, extravagant patterns are created. In the city, there are many variations of lace patterns. In the country, complicated cable patterns are knitted.

The patterns in this section focus on the cable patterns with twisted knit stitches. They appear especially prominent on a background that is often worked in reverse stockinette stitch. On wrong side rows, these stitches are knitted by purling into the back of the stitches. As patterns are created on both the right and wrong side rows, these patterns require some experience and practice in knitting. Often, a single panel is enough to give a country-style cardigan or pullover that special accent. Some of these panels are also suited for socks or knee-highs.

The knitting charts for these patterns have no edge stitches because the single panels can be combined in any way.

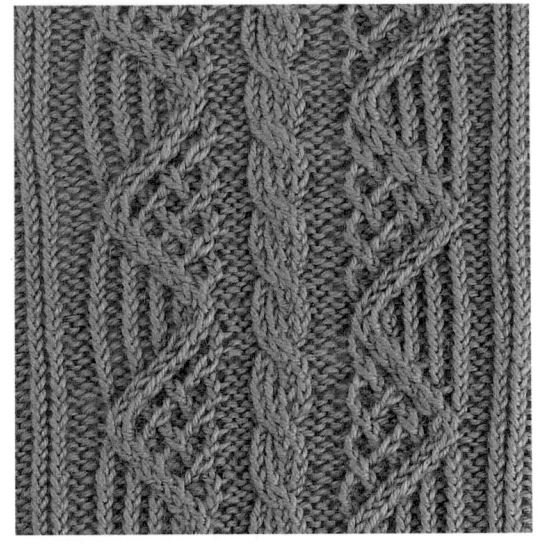

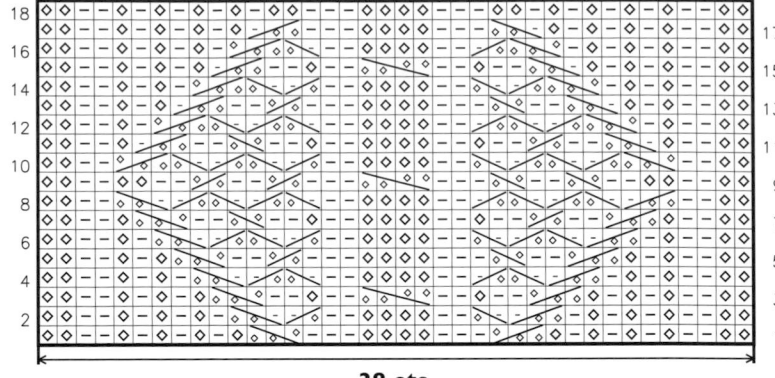

38 sts

On right and wrong side rows, knit 38 stitches according to the knitting chart. On wrong side rows, purl into the back of the stitches. On right side rows, knit into the back of the stitches. Repeat rows 1–18.

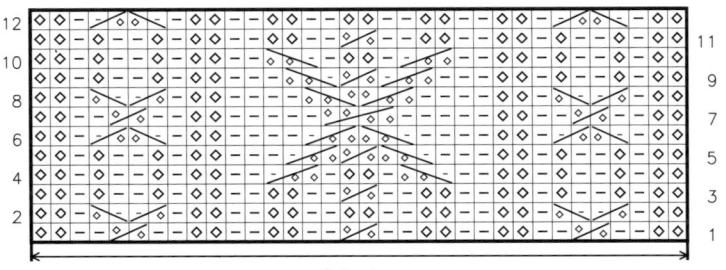

34 sts

On right and wrong side rows, knit 34 stitches according to the knitting chart. On wrong side rows, purl into the back of the stitches. On right side rows, knit into the back of the stitches. Repeat rows 1–12.

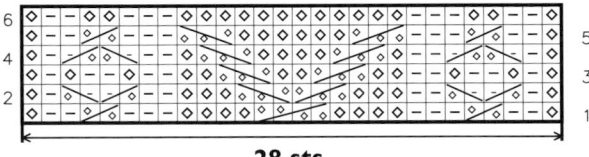

28 sts

On right and wrong side rows, knit 28 stitches according to the knitting chart. On wrong side rows, purl into the back of the stitches. On right side rows, knit into the back of the stitches. Repeat rows 1–6.

On right and wrong side rows, knit 54 stitches according to the knitting chart. On wrong side rows, purl into the back of the stitches. On right side rows, knit into the back of the stitches. Repeat rows 1–24.

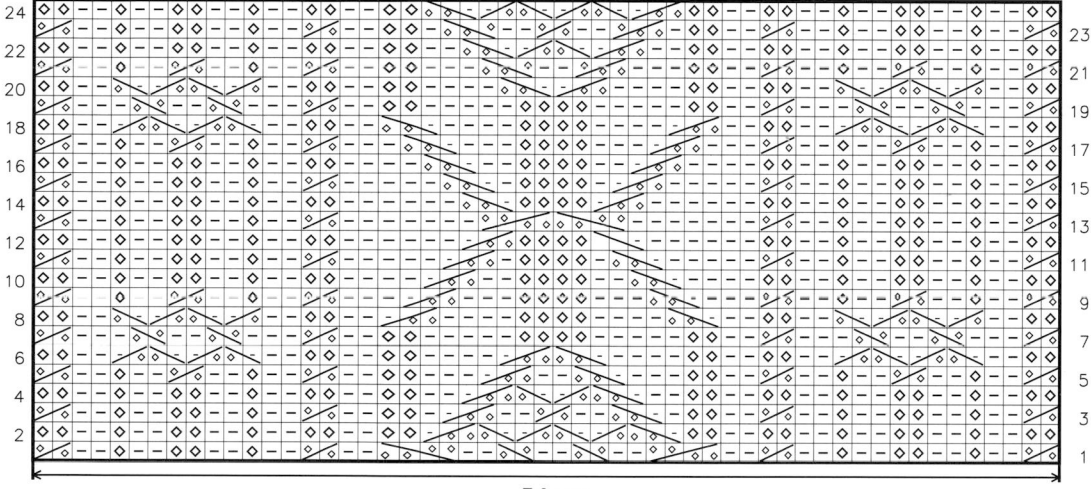

54 sts

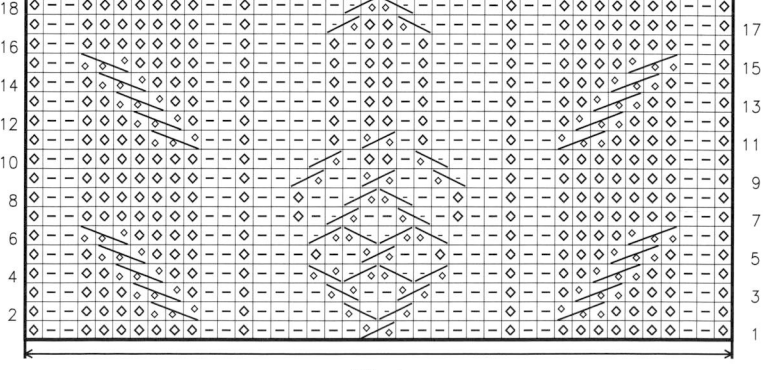

40 sts

On right and wrong side rows, knit 40 stitches according to the knitting chart. On wrong side rows, purl into the back of the stitches. On right side rows, knit into the back of the stitches. Repeat rows 1–18.

On right and wrong side rows, knit 46 stitches according to the knitting chart. On wrong side rows, purl into the back of the stitches. On right side rows, knit into the back of the stitches. Repeat rows 1–12.

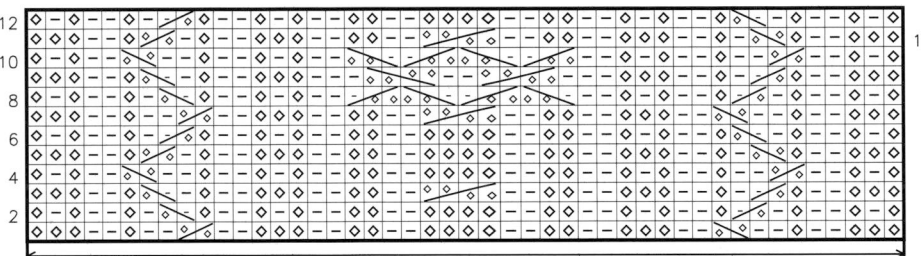

46 sts

On right and wrong side rows, knit 46 stitches according to the knitting chart. On wrong side rows, purl into the back of the stitches. On right side rows, knit into the back of the stitches. Repeat rows 1–8.

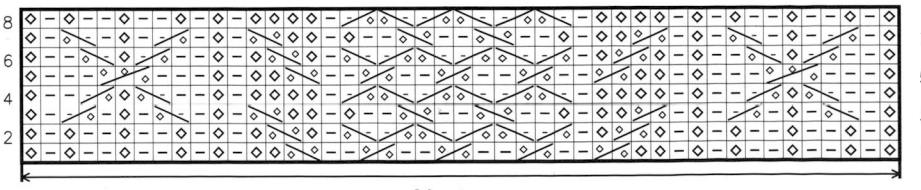

46 sts

On right and wrong side rows, knit 46 stitches according to the knitting chart. On wrong side rows, purl into the back of the stitches. On right side rows, knit into the back of the stitches. Repeat rows 1–20.

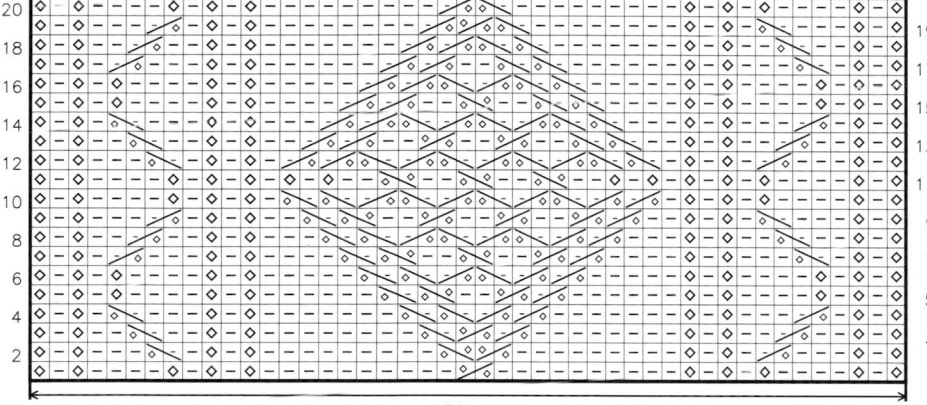

46 sts

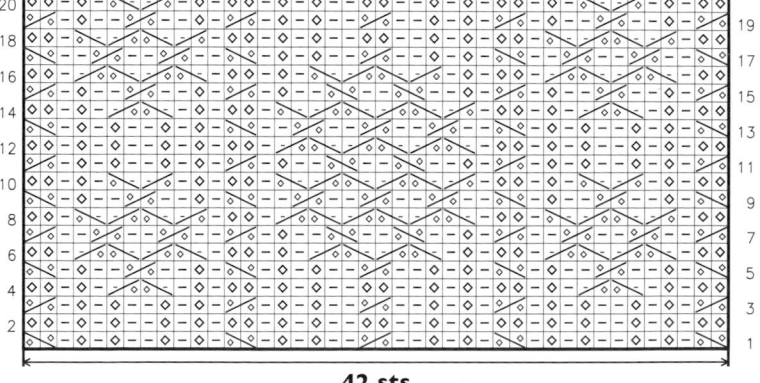

42 sts

On right and wrong side rows, knit 42 stitches according to the knitting chart. On wrong side rows, purl into the back of the stitches. On right side rows, knit into the back of the stitches. Repeat rows 1–20.

Patterns from the Alpine Region

On right and wrong side rows, knit 48 stitches according to the knitting chart. On wrong side rows, purl into the back of the stitches. On right side rows, knit into the back of the stitches. Repeat rows 1–24.

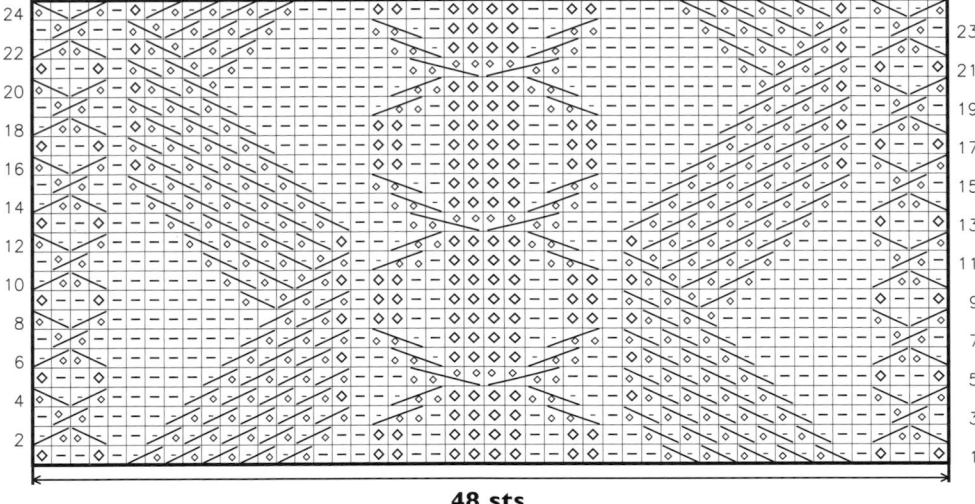

48 sts

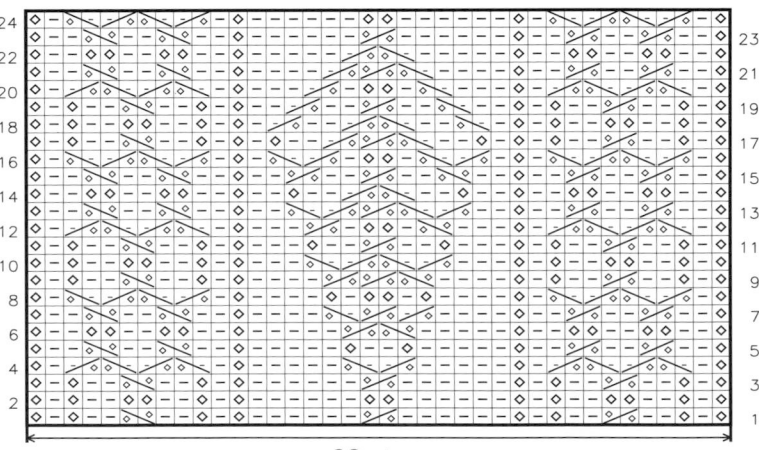

38 sts

On right and wrong side rows, knit 38 stitches according to the knitting chart. On wrong side rows, purl into the back of the stitches. On right side rows, knit into the back of the stitches. Repeat rows 1–24.

Aran Isle Patterns

Aran Isle patterns consist of cables but can include bobbles as well as variations of knit and purl stitches. Many Aran patterns are from the Irish Galway Bay, which has had a long and rich knitting tradition. Because the inhabitants in this group of islands are mostly farmers and fishermen, they needed warm and durable clothes for their work. It was only practical to make their own sweaters for this purpose. The women spun the yarn and the men usually knitted the sweaters. The origins of their sophisticated patterns can only be speculated, but it is assumed that they come from a Celtic tradition. What is more certain is that the knitters probably drew their inspiration from their work and setting. For example, twisted and cable strands reflect the daily riggings at sea, or a trellis with the diamond patterns made of twisted stitches brings to mind the embankments of stone that surrounded the fields against the rough sea winds.

Just as with Aran patterns, the patterns from the eastern coast of England are similarly rich in tradition. In Guernsey and other Channel Islands, the patterns have been handed down from generation to generation. Reverse stockinette diamonds that overlap, zigzag lines, vertical beading patterns, and simple cables are among them.

Aran Isle Patterns

Knit the side pattern on both sides of the 24-stitch middle pattern. Following the edge stitch, begin as indicated in the chart, repeat the pattern of 28 stitches, then knit the 6 stitches up to the middle pattern and the middle pattern. Following the middle pattern, repeat the pattern of 28 stitches of the side pattern. On wrong side rows, work stitches in pattern. Purl into back of stitches on wrong side rows and knit into back of stitches on right side rows. Purl the bobble stitches.

Following rows 1 and 2, repeat rows 3–26. But, with the 6-stitch cable, repeat rows 3–18.

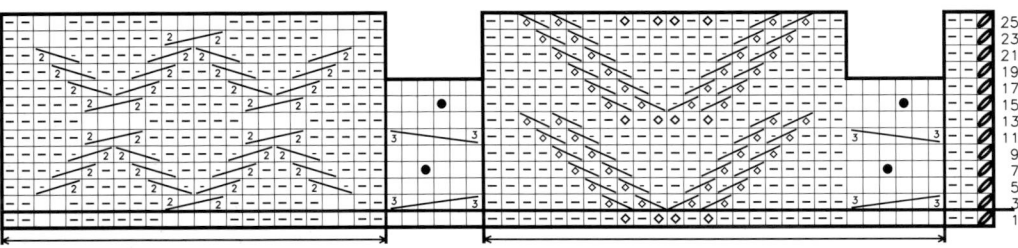

Middle Pattern: 24 sts　　**Side Pattern: 28 sts repeat**

Knit the side pattern on both sides of the 30-stitch middle pattern. On right side rows, begin with Chart B, and, following the edge stitch, repeat the pattern of 27 stitches. Knit the 30 stitches of the middle pattern according to the Chart A, then continue knitting according to Chart B beginning with Cable 1. On wrong side rows, work stitches in pattern. Following rows 1 and 2, repeat rows 3–26.

Chart A

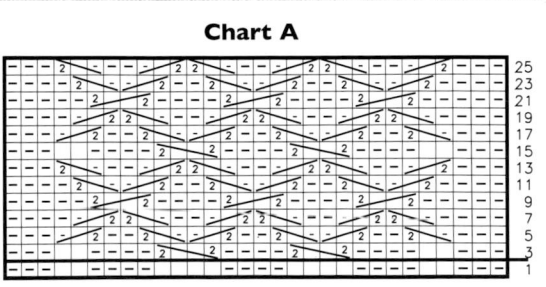

Middle Pattern: 30 sts

Chart B

Cable 1

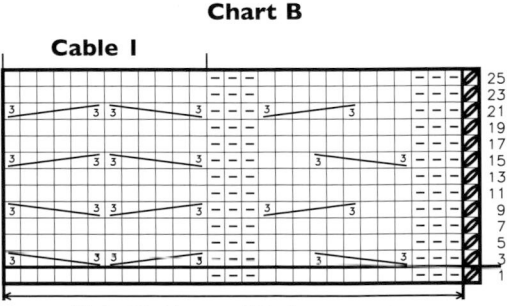

Side Pattern: 27 sts repeat

Knit the side pattern on both sides of the middle pattern.

On right side rows, following the edge stitch, repeat the pattern of 18 stitches of the side pattern according to Chart A. Knit the 22 stitches of the middle pattern, continue to knit the 21 stitches of the middle pattern according to Chart B and then edge stitch. On wrong side rows, work stitches in pattern, purling into back of stitches on wrong side rows and knitting into back of stitches on right side rows. Following rows 1 and 2, repeat rows 3–38.

MS = Middle Stitch

Chart A

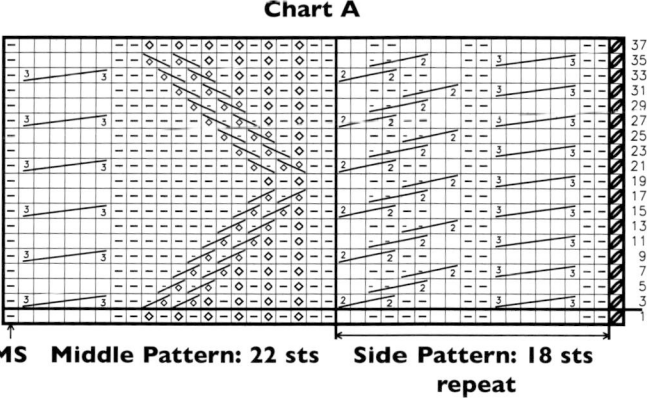

MS   Middle Pattern: 22 sts   Side Pattern: 18 sts repeat

Chart B

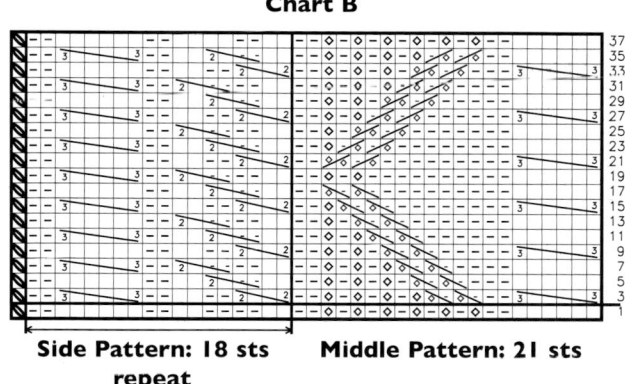

Side Pattern: 18 sts repeat   Middle Pattern: 21 sts

Panel of 41 sts + 16 + 2 edge sts

On right side rows, work according to the knitting chart. Beginning as indicated in the chart, repeat the pattern of 41 stitches and end as drawn. On wrong side rows, work stitches in pattern; purl into back of stitches on wrong side rows and knit into back of stitches on right side rows; knit the bobble stitches adjusted to the pattern or purl in stockinette strips. Repeat rows 1–24.

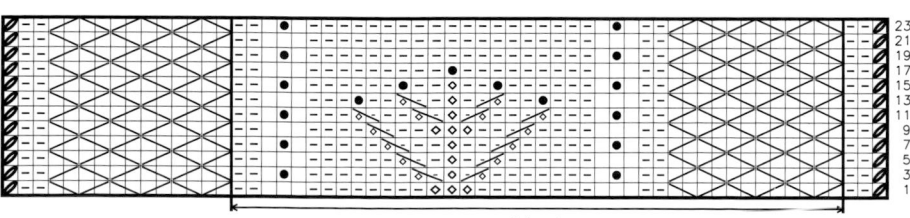

41 sts

Knit the side pattern on both sides of the middle pattern.

On right side rows, before the middle pattern and following the edge stitch, begin the side pattern as indicated in Chart B. Repeat the pattern of 4 stitches and end with 1 reverse stockinette. Then knit the middle pattern of 65 stitches according to Chart A and once more the side pattern according to Chart B. On wrong side rows, work stitches in pattern.

Chart A: Following rows 1 and 2, repeat rows 3–20.

Chart B: Following rows 1 and 2, repeat rows 3–6.

Chart A for the Middle Pattern

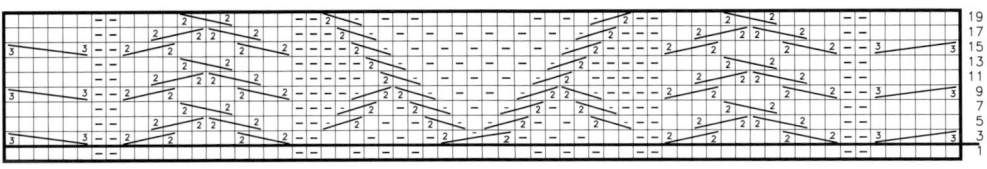

65 sts

Chart B for the Side Pattern

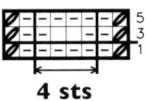

4 sts

Panel of 44 sts + 10 + 2 edge sts

On right side rows, work according to the knitting chart. Beginning as indicated in the chart, repeat the pattern of 44 stitches and end as drawn. On wrong side rows, work stitches in pattern. Repeat rows 1–36.

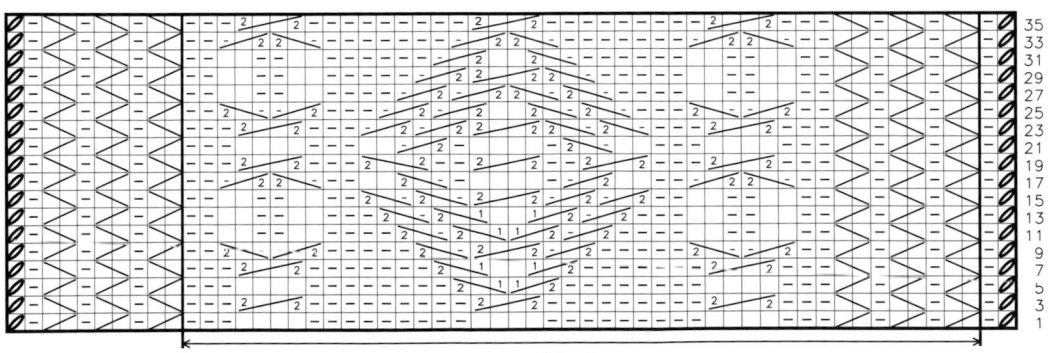

44 sts

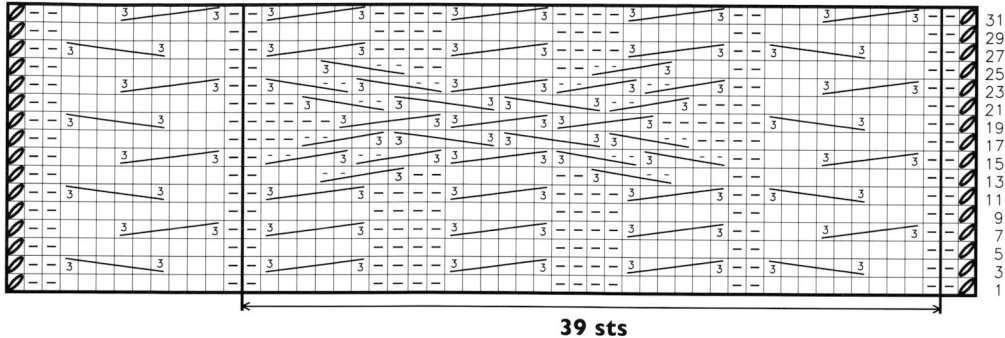

39 sts

Panel of 39 sts + 13 + 2 edge sts

On right side rows, work according to the knitting chart. Beginning as indicated in the chart, repeat the pattern of 39 stitches and end as drawn. On wrong side rows, work stitches in pattern. Repeat rows 1–32.

Panel of 52 sts + 2 edge sts

On right side rows, work according to the knitting chart. Following the edge stitch, repeat the pattern of 52 stitches and then edge stitch. On wrong side rows, work stitches in pattern. Repeat rows 1–36.

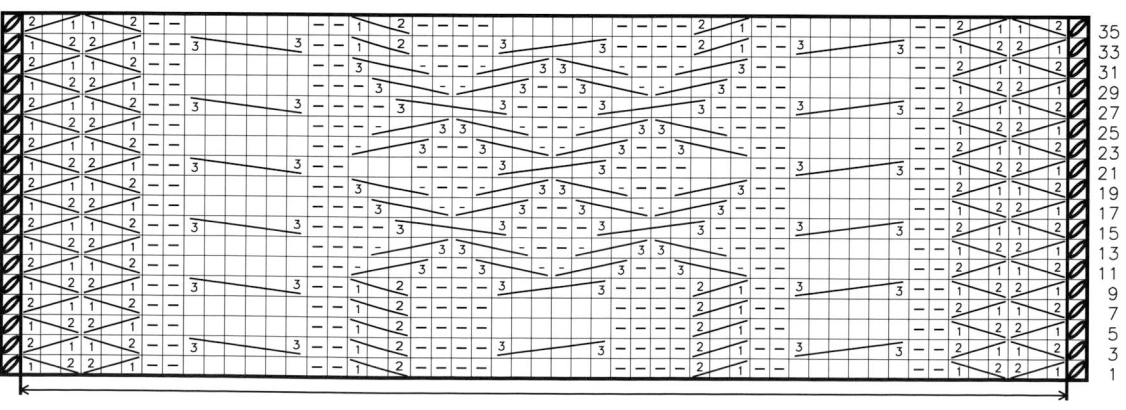

52 sts

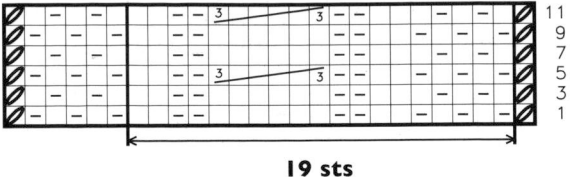

19 sts

Panel of 19 sts + 5 + 2 edge sts

On right side rows, work according to the knitting chart. Following the edge stitch, repeat the pattern of 19 stitches and end as drawn. On wrong side rows, work stitches in pattern. Repeat rows 1–12.

Multiple of 35 sts + 9 + 2 edge sts

On right and wrong side rows, work according to the knitting chart. Beginning as indicated in the chart, repeat the pattern of 35 stitches and end as drawn. Repeat rows 1–12.

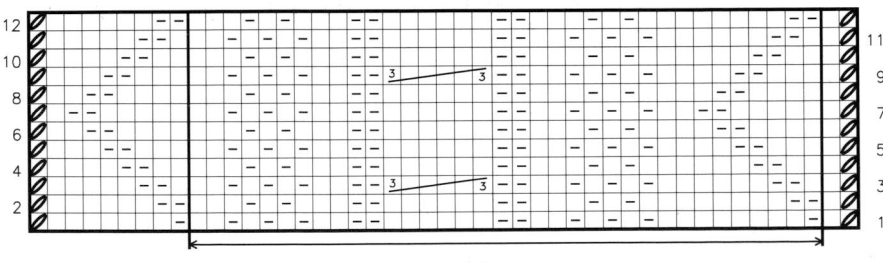

35 sts

Panel of 46 sts + 7 + 2 edge sts

On right and wrong side rows, work according to the knitting chart. Beginning as indicated in the chart, repeat the pattern of 46 stitches and end as drawn. Repeat rows 1–12.

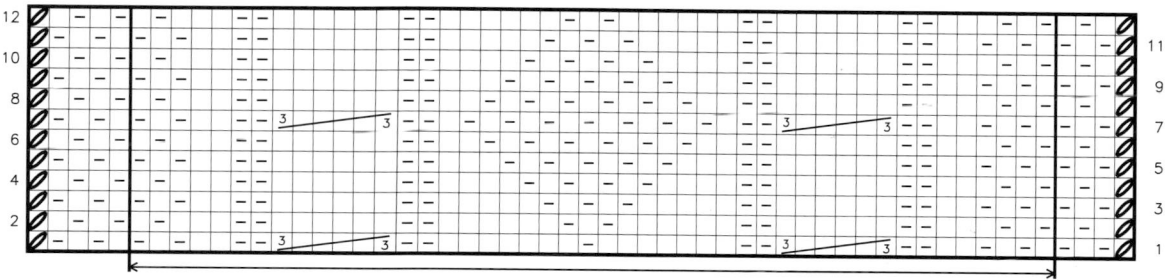

46 sts

Panel of 41 sts + 6 + 2 edge sts

On right and wrong side rows, work according to the knitting chart. Beginning as indicated in the chart, repeat the pattern of 41 stitches and end as drawn. Repeat rows 1–8.

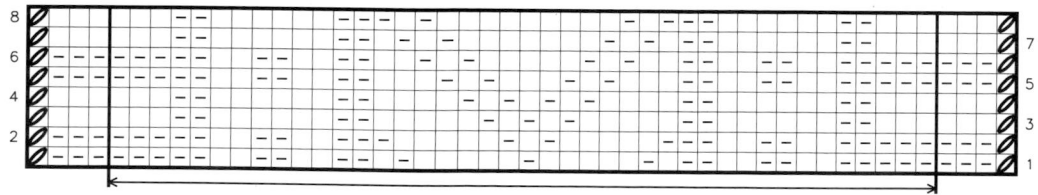

41 sts

Aran Isle Patterns

Panel of 46 sts + 7 + 2 edge sts

On right and wrong side rows, work according to the knitting chart. Beginning as indicated in the chart, repeat the pattern of 46 stitches and end as drawn. Repeat rows 1–32.

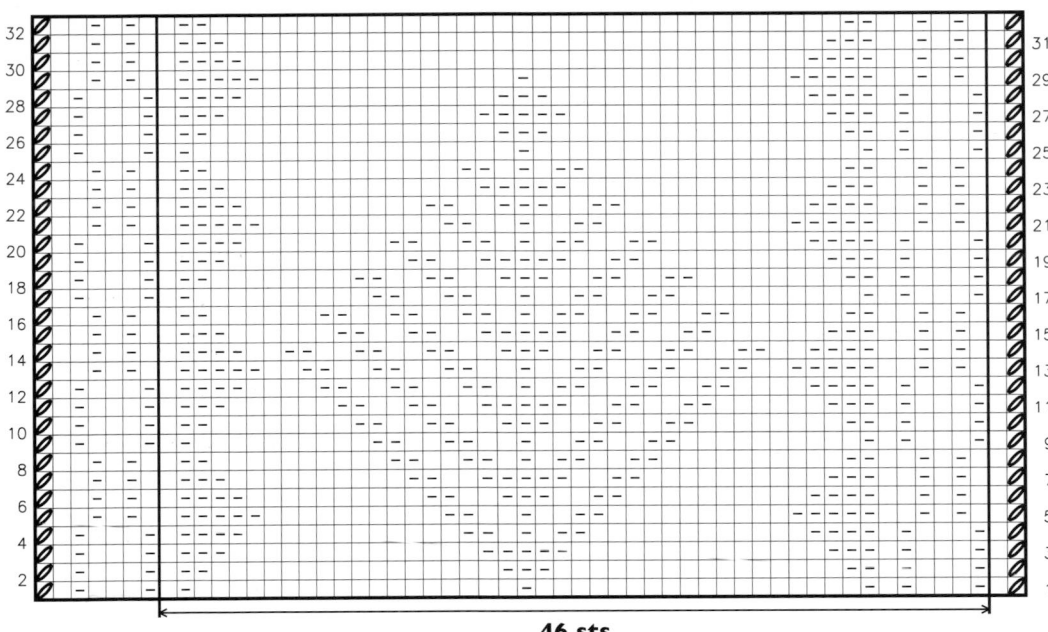

46 sts

Instead of crocheting, you can use your knitting needles to make lace trimmings or hems for garments, handkerchiefs, and blankets. When you are knitting lace, after the first cast on, purl a wrong side row before beginning the actual pattern. Most laces are arranged in such a way that you can purl all the stitches on the wrong side rows without having to pay attention to the pattern. The edge stitches are slipped at the beginning of each row with the yarn in front of the stitch. At the end of each row, the edge stitches are purled. The edge stitches must be knitted particularly tight in the decreased rows of the corners so that there will be no large holes.

With wider laces, a corner solution with decreased rows is given for the straight trimming. A knitting chart is included if you wish to trim a square blanket with lace. With narrow laces, just neatly spread out the corner and then slightly gather in the edge.

The **decreased rows for corners** are worked as follows: In each 2nd row, knit 1 stitch less than indicated in the chart (which means that you knit in row 1 of the corner up to the very last stitch); the last stitch remains unknitted on the needle. Turn the work and knit back by slipping the 1st stitch purlwise (yarn in front of stitch) and hold the yarn tightly. In the following row, knit 1 stitch less again, turn and knit back. You will now have 2 unknitted stitches on the needle. Repeat these decreased rows as long as indicated in the knitting chart. Upon reaching the corner, knit the previously unknitted stitches: In row 1, following the corner, knit the stitches of the last

Lace Trimming and Patchwork Patterns

decreased row and the following unknitted stitch, then turn the work and knit back as before. Repeat until you knit once again with all stitches.

Knitted patchwork is especially good for blankets and pillow shams. It can also be used for making extravagant vests and jackets. Squares are often knitted in rounds on 4 double-pointed needles. The individual sections are then sewn on together with stitches or crochet. This patchwork technique comes in handy especially when you are making large blankets. Working in small sections will save you from carrying the weight of the entire blanket on your needles. You will be able to use up a lot of leftover yarn when you make patchwork blankets. But to keep the blanket from becoming too colorful, it is best to use neutral color yarns to join the individual sections. You can also use the neutral color to knit some single squares as connecting elements or crochet some rounds around each square before joining them.

Lace Trimming and Patchwork Patterns

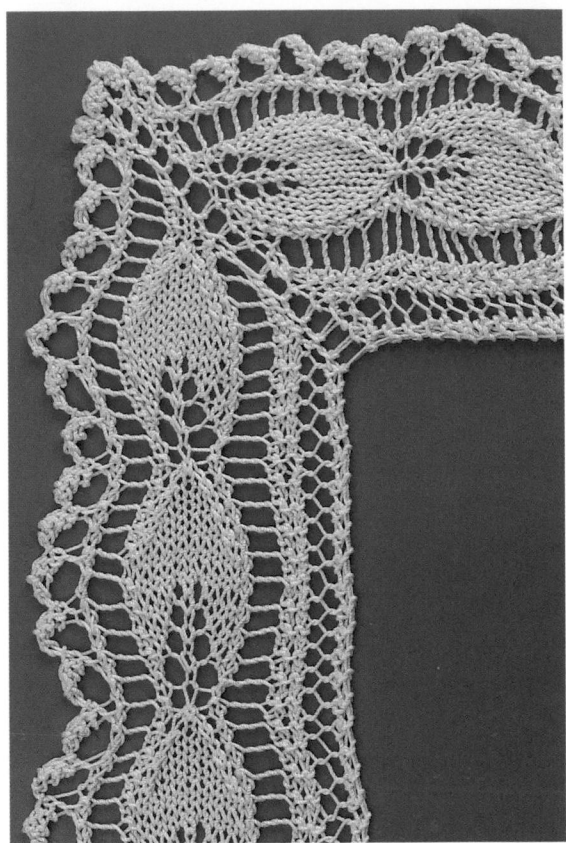

Cast on 15 stitches and knit according to Chart 1 on right and wrong side rows. Row 1 is a wrong side row. On wrong side rows, purl all stitches and yarn overs. From the double yarn over, purl 1 stitch and then knit 1 stitch. From the triple yarn over, purl 1 stitch, then knit 1 stitch and purl 1 stitch once more. Following row 1, repeat rows 2–21.

Work the corners with decreased rows according to Chart 2. They begin with pattern row 9 (= row 1 of the corners). Knit once more rows 1–54.

Chart 2

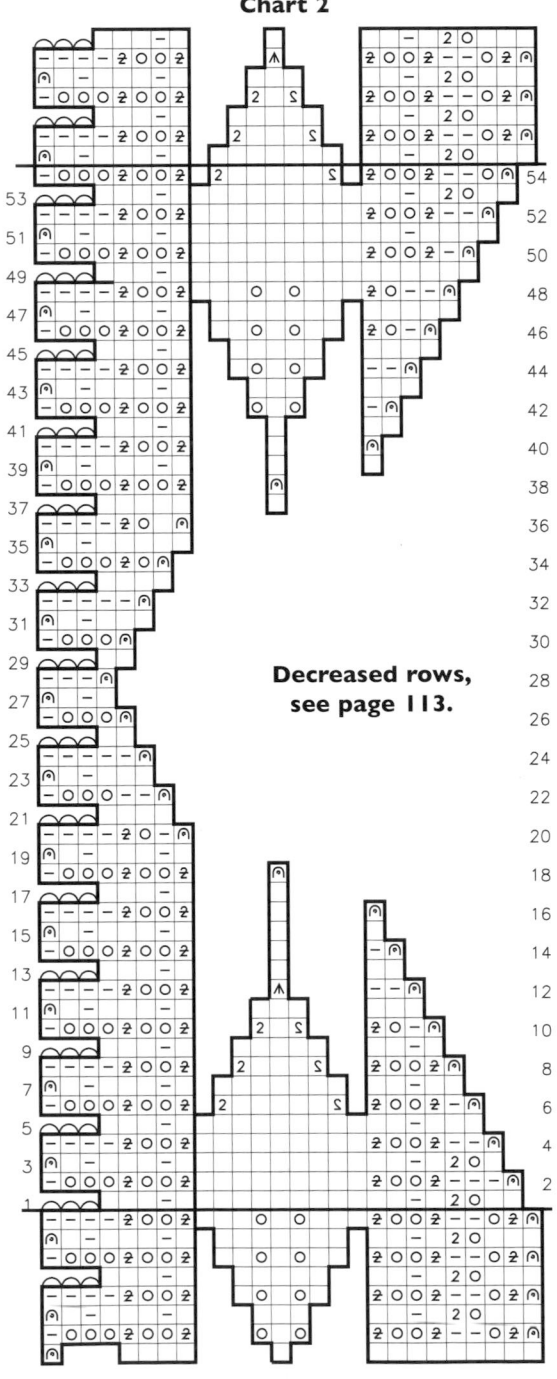

Decreased rows, see page 113.

Chart 1

15 sts

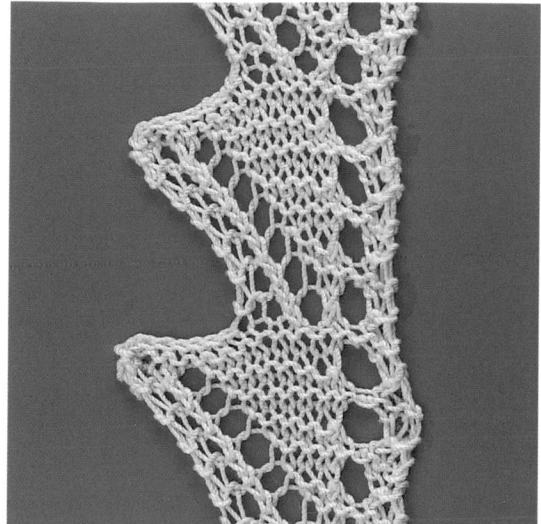

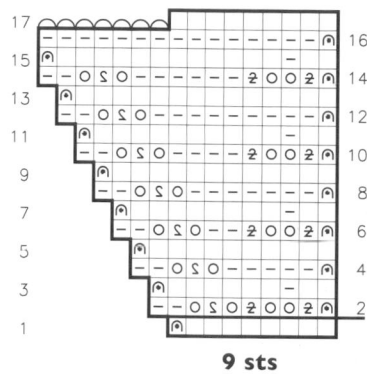

9 sts

Cast on 9 stitches and work according to knitting chart on right and wrong side rows. Row 1 is a wrong side row. On wrong side rows, purl all stitches and yarn overs; purl 1 stitch and then knit 1 stitch from the double yarn over. Following row 1, repeat rows 2–17.

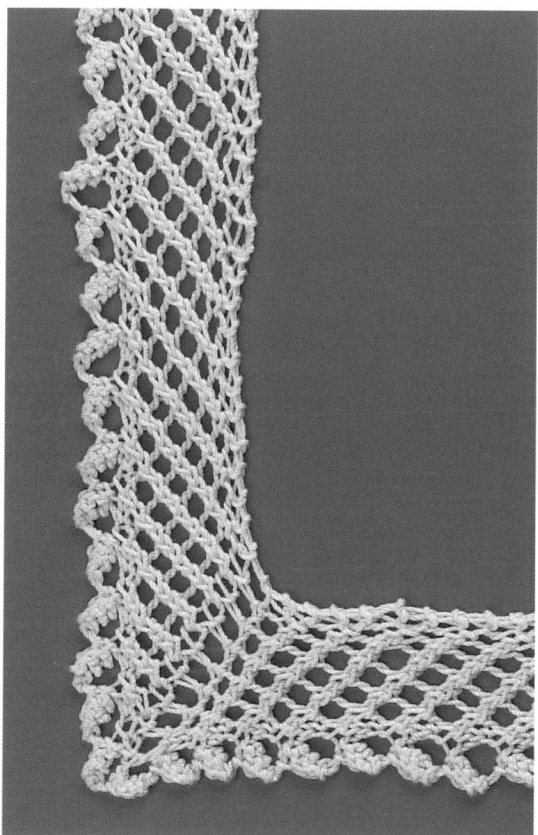

Cast on 10 stitches and work according to the knitting chart on right and wrong side rows. Row 1 is a wrong side row. On wrong side rows, purl all stitches and yarn overs; work 1 purl stitch, 1 knit stitch, and 1 purl stitch from the triple yarn over. Following row 1, repeat rows 2–5.

Work the corners with decreased rows as indicated in the chart. They begin with pattern row 3 (= row 1 of the corners). Knit once more rows 1–34.

Decreased rows, see page 113.

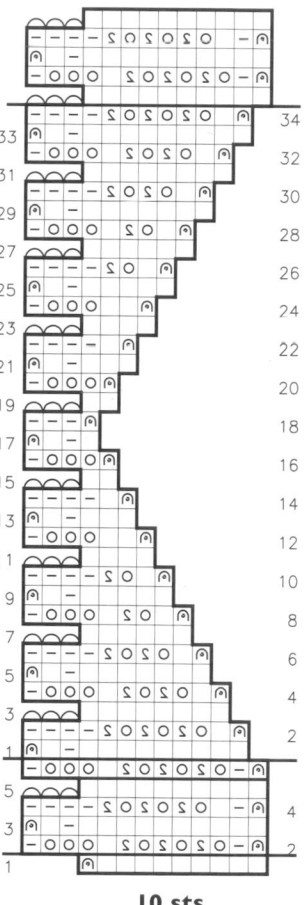

10 sts

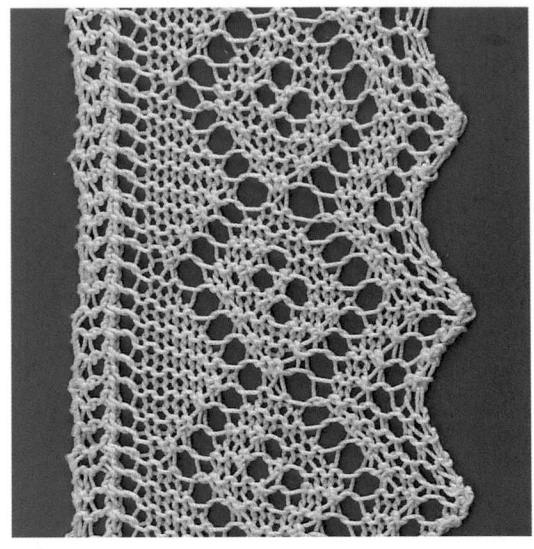

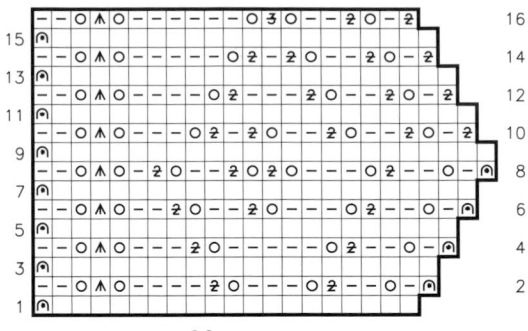

20 sts

Cast on 20 stitches and work according to the knitting chart on right and wrong side rows. Row 1 is a wrong side row. On wrong side rows, purl all stitches and yarn overs. Repeat rows 1–16.

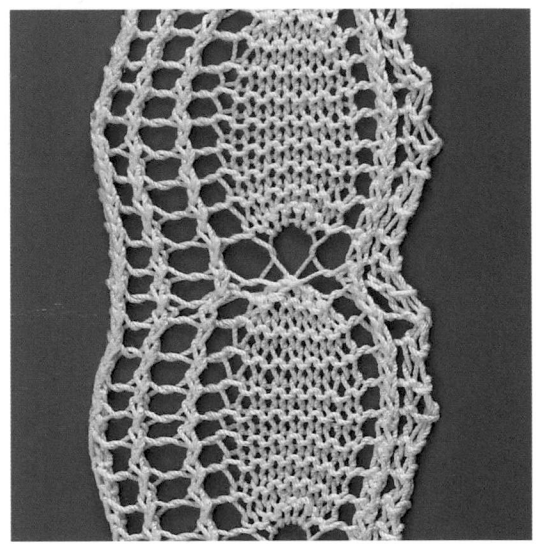

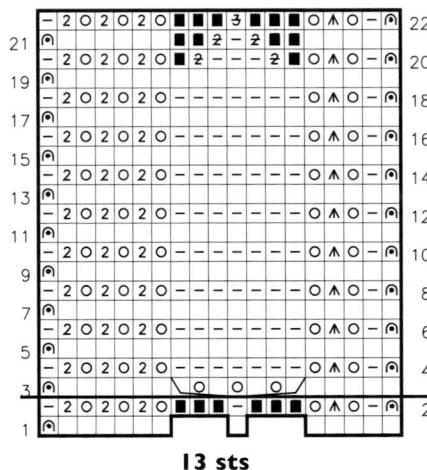

13 sts

Cast on 13 stitches and work according to the knitting chart on right and wrong side rows. Row 1 is a wrong side row. On wrong side rows, purl all stitches and yarn overs. Following rows 1 and 2, repeat rows 3–22.

 = Work 7 stitches in 1 stitch (alternate 1 purl stitch, 1 yarn over).

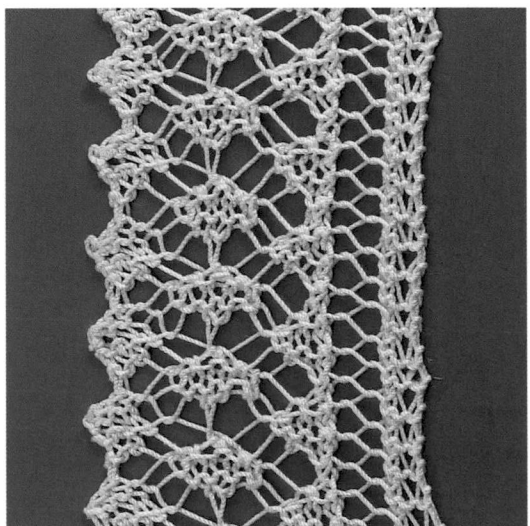

14 sts

Cast on 14 stitches and work according to the knitting chart on right and wrong side rows. Row 1 is a wrong side row. On wrong side rows, purl all stitches and yarn overs, or purl together the corresponding stitches. Following row 1, repeat rows 2–7.

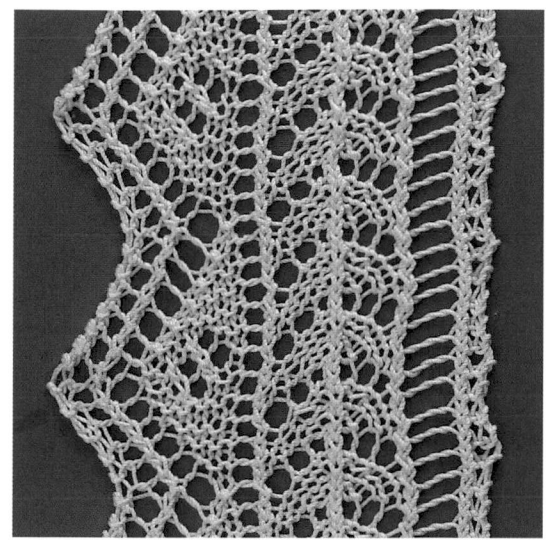

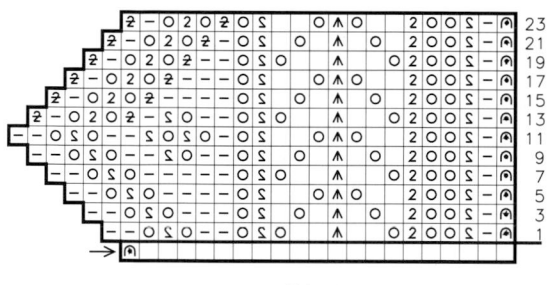

21 sts

Cast on 21 stitches and purl 1 wrong side row. Work right side rows according to the knitting chart. On wrong side rows, purl all stitches and yarn overs. Following the wrong side row, repeat rows 1–24.

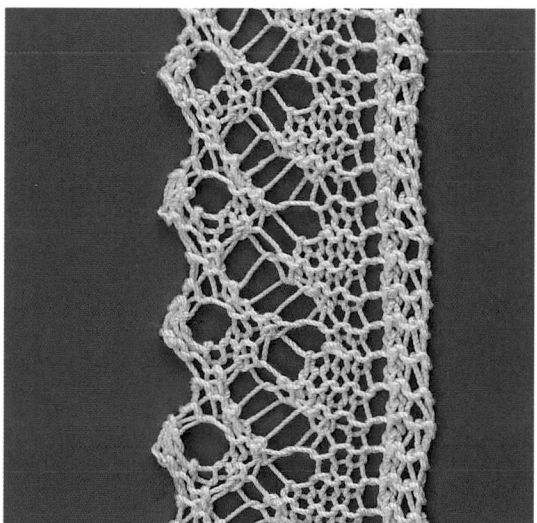

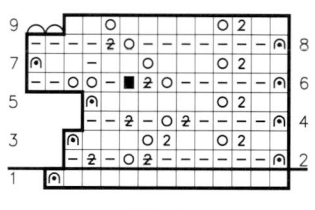

13 sts

Cast on 13 stitches and work according to the knitting chart on right and wrong side rows. Row 1 is a wrong side row. On wrong side rows, purl all stitches and yarn overs, or purl together the corresponding stitches. In row 7, purl 1 stitch and then knit 1 stitch from the 2 yarn overs as indicated in the chart. Following row 1, repeat rows 2–9.

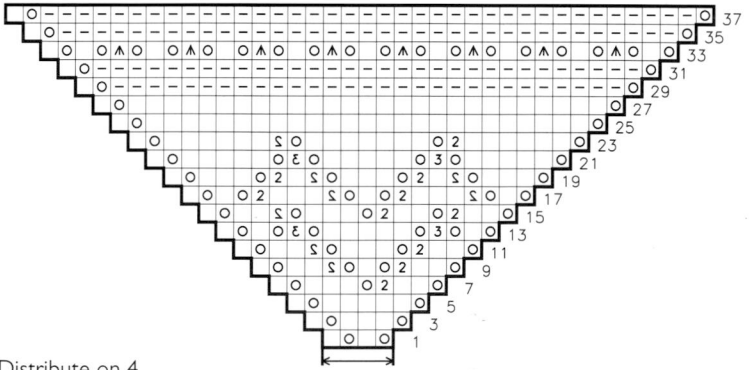

Distribute on 4 double-pointed needles 8 cast-on stitches (2 stitches per needle) and knit 1 round. Then work in odd rounds according to the knitting chart. The pattern repeats 4 times. In even rounds, knit all stitches and yarn overs. Knit once more rounds 1–38.

Lace Trimming and Patchwork Patterns

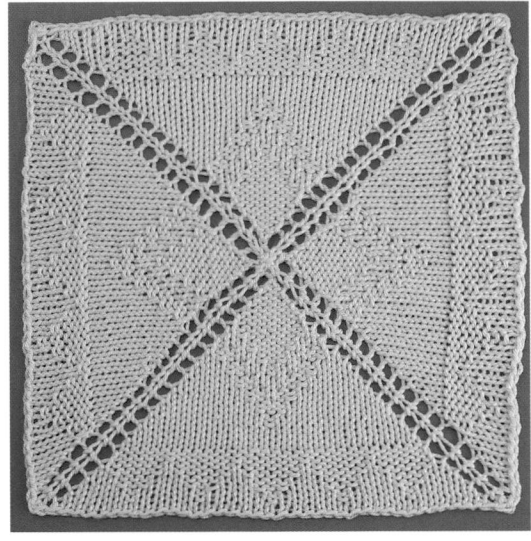

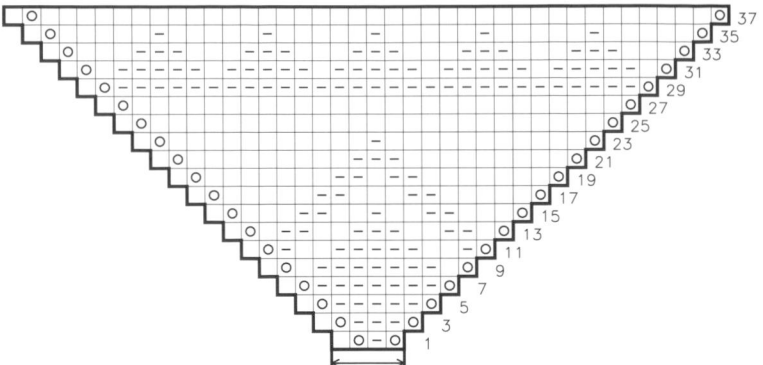

Distribute on 4 double-pointed needles 8 cast-on stitches (2 stitches per needle) and knit 1 round. Then work in odd rounds according to the knitting chart. The pattern repeats 4 times. In even rounds, work stitches in pattern and knit the yarn overs. Knit once more rounds 1–38.

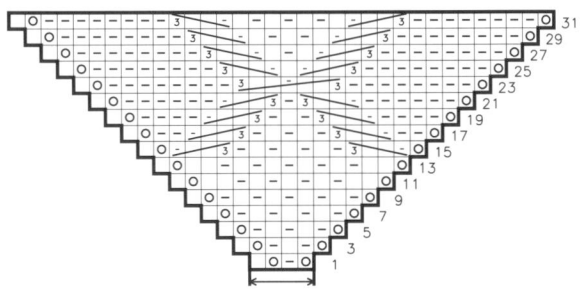

Distribute on 4 double-pointed needles 8 cast-on stitches (2 stitches per needle) and knit 1 round. Then work in odd rounds according to the knitting chart. The pattern repeats 4 times. In even rounds, work stitches in pattern and knit the yarn overs. Knit once more rounds 1–32.

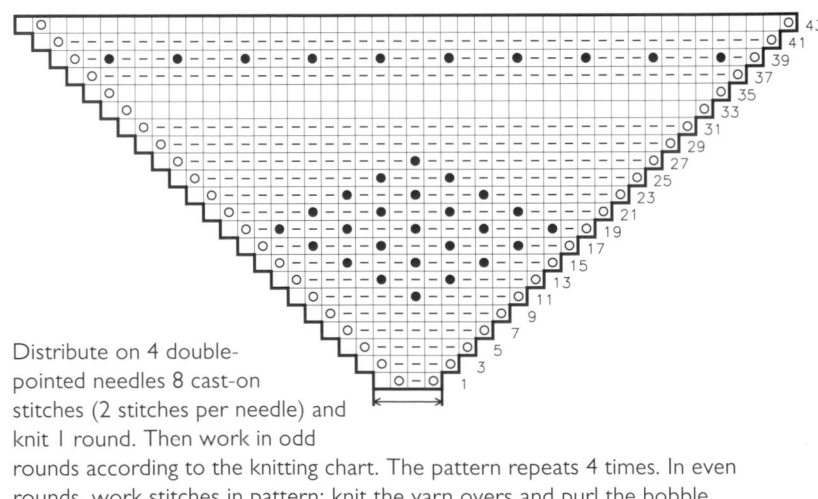

Distribute on 4 double-pointed needles 8 cast-on stitches (2 stitches per needle) and knit 1 round. Then work in odd rounds according to the knitting chart. The pattern repeats 4 times. In even rounds, work stitches in pattern; knit the yarn overs and purl the bobble stitches. Knit once more rounds 1–44.

Distribute on 4 double-pointed needles 8 cast-on stitches (2 stitches per needle) and work in odd rounds according to the knitting chart. The pattern repeats 4 times. In even rounds, work stitches in pattern and knit the yarn overs. Knit once more rounds 1–36.

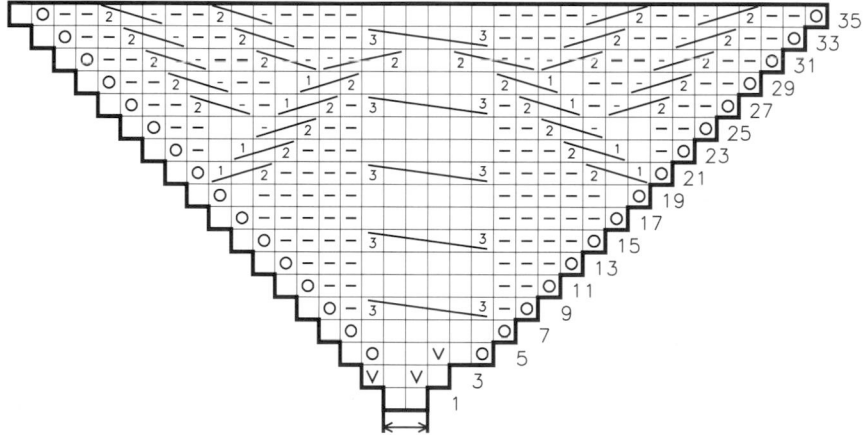

Distribute on 4 double-pointed needles 8 cast-on stitches (2 stitches per needle) and knit 1 round. Then work in odd rounds according to the knitting chart. The pattern repeats 4 times. In even rounds, work stitches in pattern and knit the yarn overs. Knit once more rounds 1–28.

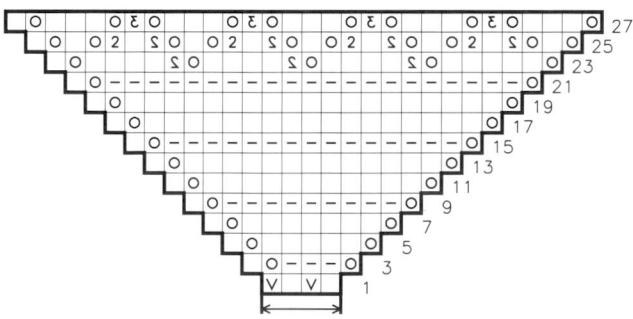

Distribute on 4 double-pointed needles 12 cast-on stitches (3 stitches per needle) and knit 1 round. Then work in odd rounds according to the knitting chart. The pattern repeats 4 times. In even rounds, work stitches in pattern and knit the yarn overs. Knit once more rounds 1–38.

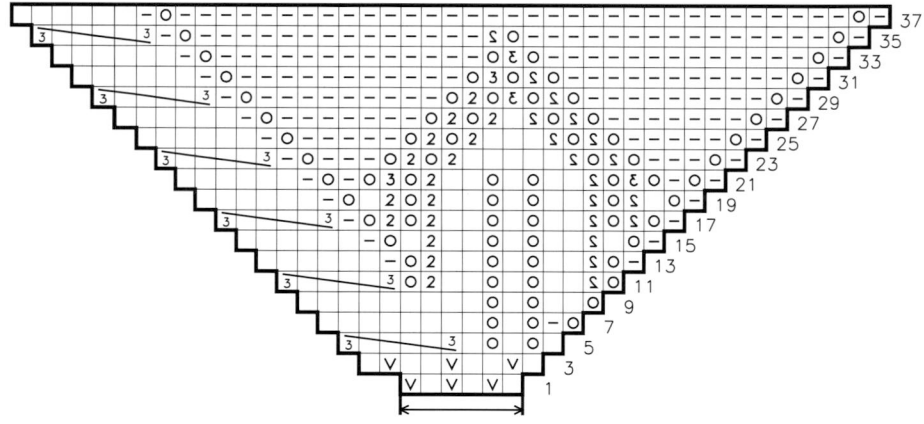

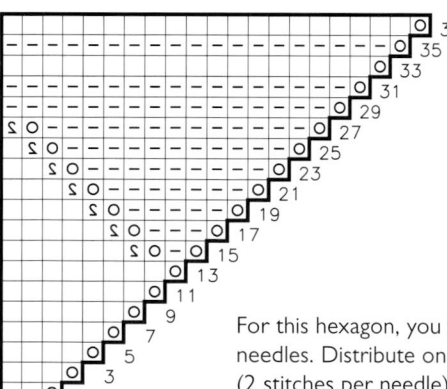

For this hexagon, you need 7 double-pointed needles. Distribute on 6 needles 12 cast-on stitches (2 stitches per needle) and work in odd rounds according to the knitting chart. The pattern repeats 6 times. In even rounds, work stitches in pattern and knit the yarn overs. Knit once more rounds 1–38.

In this section, you will find unusual patterns in various techniques. Some of the techniques may seem familiar to you from other sections in this book, but the use of extraordinary colors or additional tricks give these techniques a new twist.

Experiment with different color yarns. You will be surprised by the eye-catching clothes and cute children's outfits you make. The intarsia technique is generally applied when great color surfaces are to be placed next to each other. On page 124, you will also see that smaller motifs can be comfortably and effectively worked in this technique.

Striking designs on the neckline of sweaters or collars of cardigans can give your outfit a unique look. Try decorating your knitted project with a "fur trimming" in loop technique. You can also try mitten cuffs, or an entire muff, in this original way.

Knitting with Beads

Beadwork can produce great pieces of knitted art. Elegant purses, bags, and even mittens were created in this technique during the mid-19th century. Creating these pieces required detailed and laborious work. All the beads had to be lined up individually and in right colors on the yarn. In addition, this needed to be done in the reverse order of the knitted work.

In this section, you will find some simpler patterns with knitted-in beads that will give your project an extra finishing touch. It is important to be sure that your chosen beads can slip easily through the yarn. For yarns that are 137 to 164 yards (125 to 150 m) long and

Various Techniques

weigh 1.75 oz (50g), you will need beads that are at least 4 mm in diameter with a respectively large hole.

Before you start threading, calculate how many beads you will need. The instructions provide both the number for the pattern repeat as well as for the beginning and end of the pattern. In these patterns, the beads are only knitted in on the right side rows. Work the corresponding stitch by knitting into the back of the stitch (i.e., insert needle from right to left), hold the yarn with the bead in front of the right-hand needle, hold on to the bead, and then pass the stitch over the yarn and bead. When pulling the yarn, hold on to the bead so that it does not disappear into the wrong side of the work.

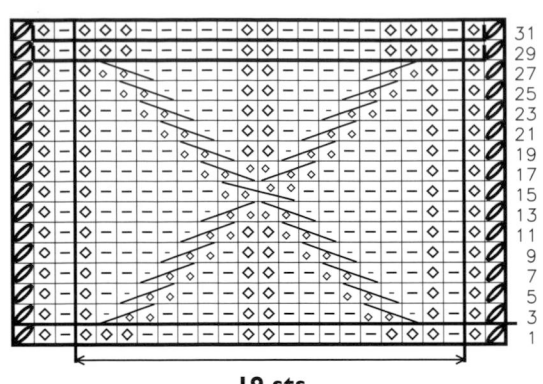

19 sts

Multiple of 19 sts + 3 + 2 edge sts

On right side rows, work according to the knitting chart. Beginning as indicated in the chart, repeat the pattern of 19 stitches and end as drawn. On wrong side rows, work stitches in pattern. On right side rows, knit into the back of stitches. On wrong side rows, purl into the back of stitches. Following rows 1 and 2, repeat rows 3–32.

⌐⌐ = In row 29 and 31, make a stitch out of the edge stitch by knitting into the back of the stitch with a double-pointed needle and keep it in front of the work. * Knit into the back of the edge stitch on the double-pointed needle, slip back onto the double-pointed needle and hold in front of work, then knit the 1st stitch of the left-hand needle as indicated in the chart; repeat from *. At the end of the row, lift the stitch on the double-pointed needle to the left-hand needle in front of the edge stitch and purl together.

Even number of stitches

Row 1 (wrong side row): Knit all stitches.

Row 2 (right side row): Edge stitch, * knit 1 stitch, then work 1 loop. For this, knit the next stitch but leave the stitch on the left-hand needle. Bring the yarn in front, ground the left thumb, and take it to the back of the needles. Stretch the loop into the desired length, then take your thumb out of the loop and hold on to it. Now knit the stitch once more and slip it off the needle, make 1 yarn over, and pass the just-knitted stitches over the yarn over. Repeat from *, edge stitch.

Row 3: Knit all stitches.

Row 4: Edge stitch, * make 1 loop, knit 1 stitch; repeat from *, edge stitch.

Repeat rows 1–4.

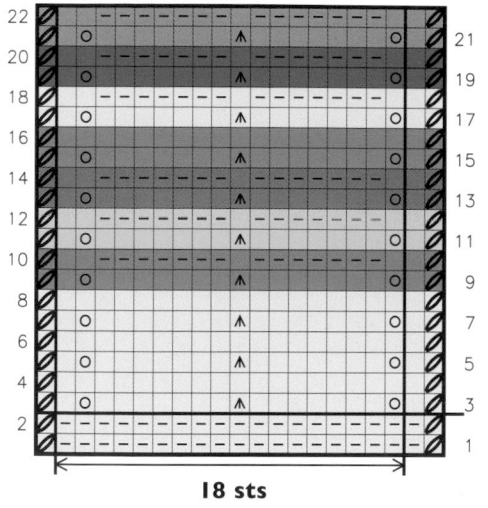

Multiple of 18 sts + 1 + 2 edge sts

On right and wrong side rows, work according to the knitting chart. Beginning as indicated in the chart, repeat the pattern of 18 stitches and then edge stitch. Following rows 1 and 2, repeat rows 3–22.

18 sts

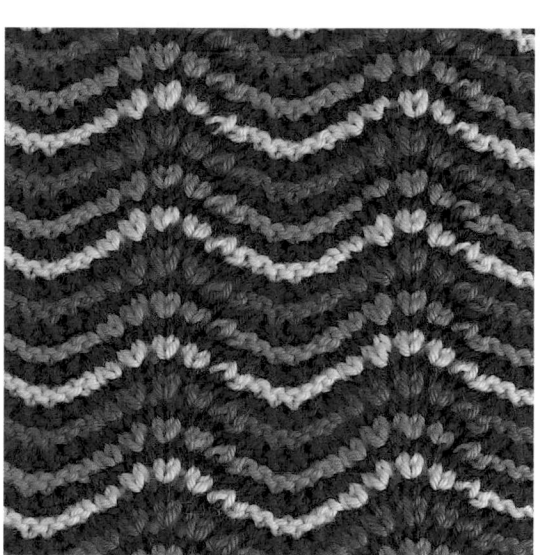

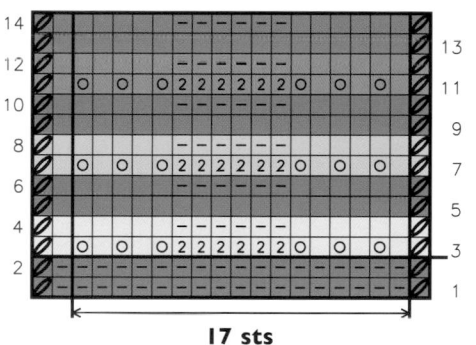

17 sts

Multiple of 17 sts + 1 + 2 edge sts

On right and wrong side rows, work according to the knitting chart. On right side rows, following the edge stitch, repeat the pattern of 17 stitches and end as drawn. Following rows 1 and 2, repeat rows 3–14.

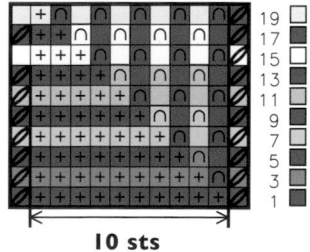

10 sts

Multiple of 10 sts + 2 edge sts

On right side rows, work according to the knitting chart. Following the edge stitch, repeat the pattern of 10 stitches and then edge stitch. On wrong side rows, knit stitches as explained in the description of symbols, slipping the slipped stitches of the right side rows with the yarn in front of stitch. Repeat rows 1–20.

The small boxes next to the row numbers indicate with which color the rows are knitted.

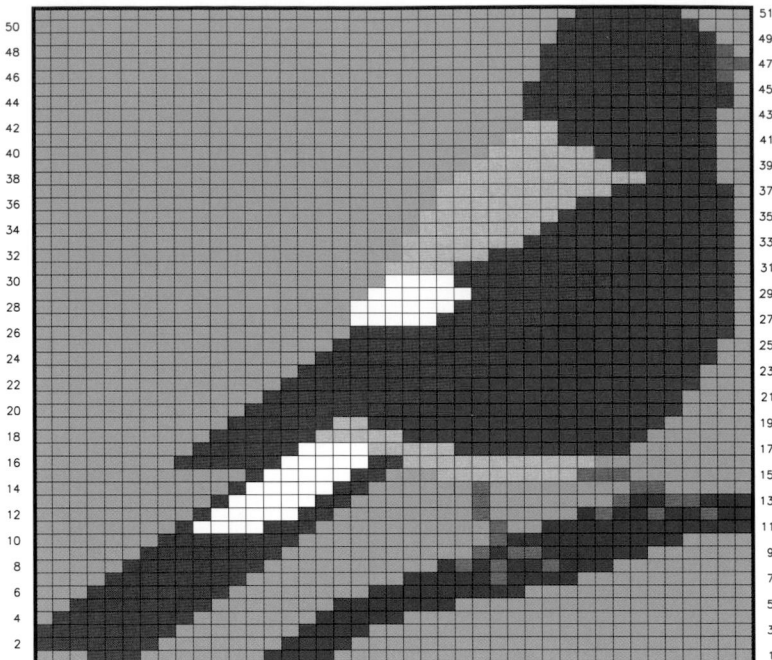

41 sts

Bullfinch: Work 41 stitches in stockinette using intarsia technique. For each color square, use an extra ball of yarn and cross the yarns with each change of color on the backside of the work so that no holes are made. Individual stitches can also be embroidered on later with grafting stitches. Knit once rows 1–51.

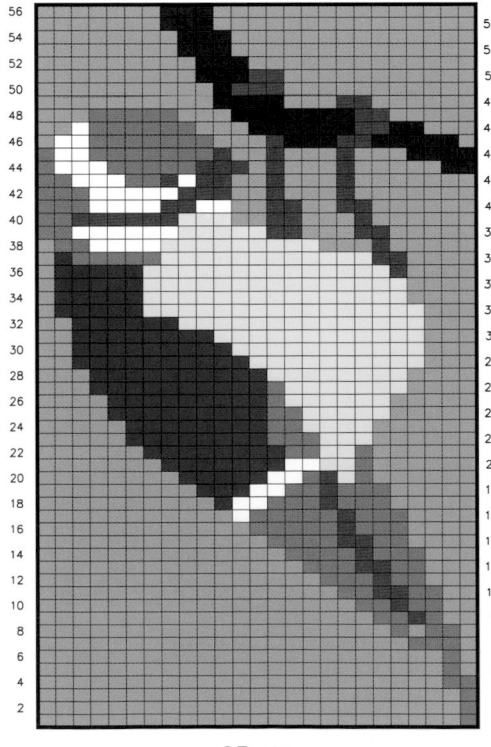

25 sts

Blue tit: Work 25 stitches in stockinette using intarsia technique. For each color square, use an extra ball of yarn and cross the yarns with each change of color on the backside of the work so that no holes are made. Individual stitches can also be embroidered on later with grafting stitches. Knit once rows 1–56.

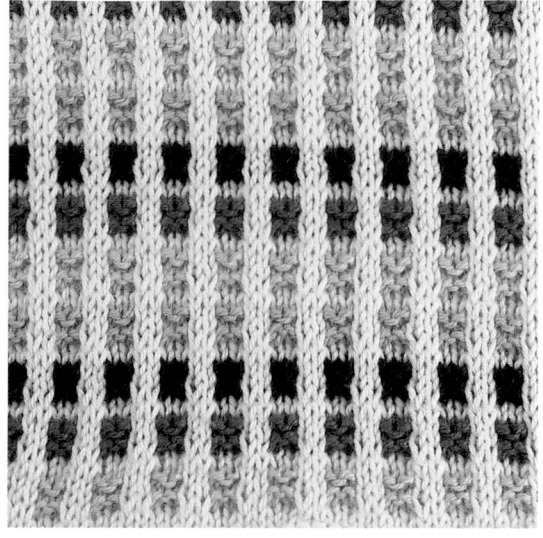

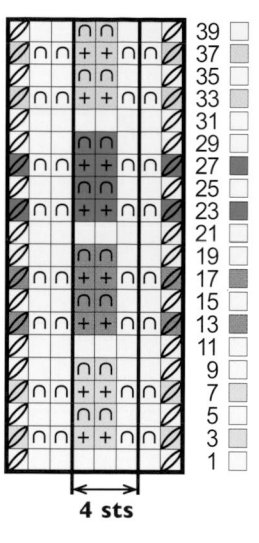

Multiple of 4 sts + 2 + 2 edge sts

On right side rows, work according to the knitting chart. Beginning as indicated in the chart, repeat the pattern of 4 stitches and end as drawn. On wrong side rows, work all knitted stitches as explained in the description of symbols, slipping the slipped stitches of the right side rows purlwise with the yarn in front of stitch.

Repeat rows 1–40.

The small boxes next to the row numbers indicate with which color the rows are knitted.

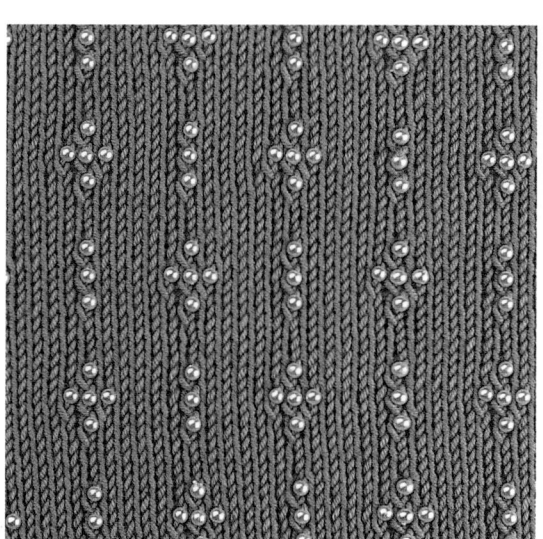

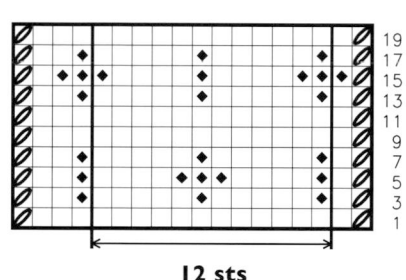

Multiple of 12 sts + 4 + 2 edge sts

Thread 16 beads per pattern repeat. For the beginning of the pattern, thread 1 bead; for the end of the pattern, thread 7 beads.

On right side rows, work according to the knitting chart. Beginning as indicated in the chart, repeat the pattern of 12 stitches and end as drawn. On wrong side rows, purl all stitches. Repeat rows 1–20.

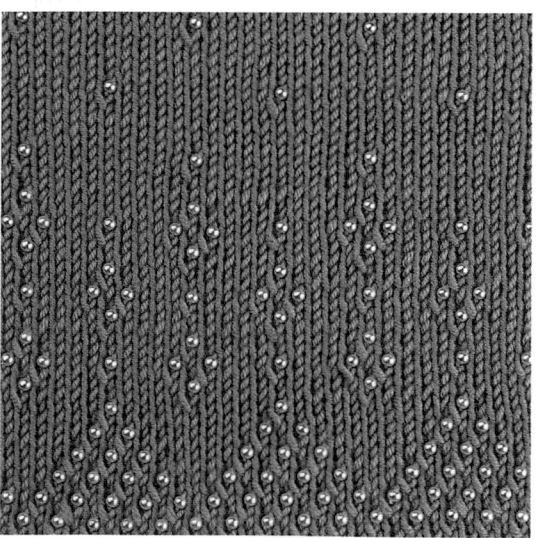

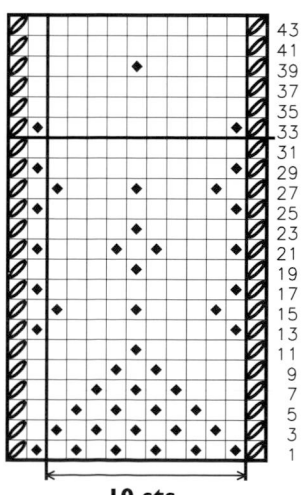

Multiple of 10 sts + 1 + 2 edge sts

Thread 35 beads for rows 1–32 per pattern repeat; for the end of the pattern, thread 6 beads. For rows 33–44, thread 2 beads per pattern repeat; for the end of the pattern, thread 1 bead.

On right side rows, work according to the knitting chart. Following the edge stitch, repeat the pattern of 10 stitches and end as drawn. On wrong side rows, purl all stitches. Knit once rows 1–32, then repeat rows 33–44.

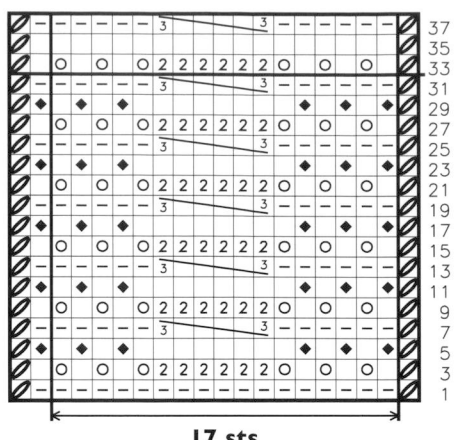

17 sts

Multiple of 17 sts + 1 + 2 edge sts

Thread 25 beads per pattern repeat; for the end of the pattern, thread 5 beads.

On right side rows, work according to the knitting chart. Following the edge stitch, repeat the pattern of 17 stitches and end as drawn. On wrong side rows, knit all stitches in pattern and purl the yarn overs. Knit once rows 1–32, then repeat rows 33–38.

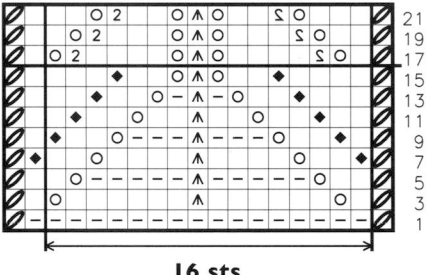

16 sts

Multiple of 16 sts + 1 + 2 edge sts

Thread 9 beads per pattern repeat; for the end of the pattern, thread 1 bead.

On right side rows, work according to the knitting chart. Following the edge stitch, repeat the pattern of 16 stitches and end as drawn. On wrong side rows, knit all stitches in pattern and purl the yarn overs. Knit once rows 1–16, then repeat rows 17–22.

A

Alpine region patterns, 99–104
   knitting charts, 99
   overview, 99
   variations, 100–104
Aran Isle patterns, 105–112
   origin, 105
   overview, 105
   reverse stockinette stitch, 105, 108
   stockinette stitch, 107
   variations, 106–112

B

Beadwork, 121, 125–126
Blue tit pattern, 124
Brioche stitch patterns, 36–44
   double Shaker knitting, 36, 37
   garter stitch and, 36
   honeycomb stitch, 39
   overview, 36
   single Shaker knitting, 38
   slip-stitch and, 36
   two-color, 37, 39
   variations, 40–44
Bullfinch pattern, 124

C

Cable patterns, 45–51
   overview, 45
   variations, 46–51

D

Double Shaker knitting, 36, 37

G

Garter stitch, 14, 36

I

Intarsia technique, 121

J

Jacquard patterns, 71–81
   "float," 71
   overview, 71
   variations, 72–81

K

Key, charts/patterns, 8–12
Knit and purl stitch patterns, 13–30
   garter stitch, 14, 36
   overview, 13
   reverse stockinette stitch, 14
   stockinette stitch, 14
   variations, 14–30
Knitting charts key, 8–12
Knitting, The history of, 6–7
Knitting into stitches, 94–98
   described, 94
   lace patterns, 94
   reverse stockinette stitch, 96, 98
   slip-stitch patterns, 94, 95
   variations, 95–98
   yarn types, 94
Knitting machine, 7

L

Lace patterns, 52–62
   knitting into stitches, 94
   overview, 52
   variations, 53–62
   yarn types, 52
Lace trimming/patchwork patterns, 113–120
   overview, 113
   variations, 114–120
Lee, William, 7

M

Minipatterns, 82–86
   overview, 82
   variations, 83–86
   yarn types, 82

N

Norwegian patterns. *See* Jacquard patterns

O

Openwork patterns, 63–70
   overview, 63
   variations, 64–70

Index

P

Patchwork. *See* Lace trimming/patchwork patterns
Pattern keys, 8–12
Purl. *See* Knit and purl stitch patterns

R

Reverse stockinette stitch, 14
Rib patterns, 31–35
   defined, 31
   variations, 32–35

S

Single Shaker knitting, 38
Slip-stitch patterns, 87–93
   brioche stitch and, 36
   knitting into stitches, 94, 95

overview, 87
variations, 88–93
yarn types, 87
Stockinette stitch, 14

T

Two-color double Shaker knitting, 37

V

Various techniques
   beadwork, 121, 125–126
   overview, 121
   patterns, 122–126

Knitting Needles

US	Metric	UK
0	2mm	14
1	2.25mm	13
	2.5mm	
2	2.75mm	12
	3mm	11
3	3.25mm	10
4	3.5mm	
5	3.75mm	9
6	4mm	8
7	4.5mm	7
8	5mm	6
9	5.5mm	5
10	6mm	4
10.5	6.5mm	3
	7mm	2
	7.5mm	1
11	8mm	0
13	9mm	00
15	10mm	000

Metric Equivalents

Inches	Centimeters	Inches	Centimeters
.25	.6	12	30.5
.50	1.3	13	33.0
.75	1.9	14	35.6
1	2.5	15	38.1
1.25	3.2	16	40.6
1.5	3.8	17	43.2
1.75	4.4	18	45.7
2	5.1	19	48.3
2.5	6.4	20	50.8
3	7.6	21	53.3
3.5	8.9	22	55.9
4	10.2	23	58.4
4.5	11.4	24	61.0
5	12.7	25	63.5
6	15.2	26	66.0
7	17.8	27	68.6
8	20.3	28	71.1
9	22.9	29	73.7
10	25.4	30	76.2
11	27.9		